GOVERNMENT OFFICE FOR THE SOUTH EAST
GOVERNMENT OFFICE FOR EAST OF ENGLAND
GOVERNMENT OFFICE FOR LONDON

Regional Planning Guidance
for the South East (RPG 9)

DETR

ENVIRONMENT
TRANSPORT
REGIONS

March 2001

London: The Stationery Office

Government Office for the South East
Bridge House
1 Walnut Tree Close
Guildford
GU1 4GA
Telephone 01483 884824 or 882516
Internet service http://www.go-se.gov.uk/infor/planning-HTML

ISBN 0 11753562 1

Printed in Great Britain for The Stationery Office on material containing 75% post-consumer waste and 25% ECF pulp.
March 2001

TJ003602 C15 03/01 9385 14315

Contents

Chapter 1

Introduction

1.1   This *Regional Planning Guidance for the South East* (RPG9) is provided by the Secretary of State for the Environment, Transport and the Regions. It covers the period up to 2016 setting the framework for the longer term future. This guidance supersedes the *Regional Planning Guidance for the South East* issued in March 1994, which covered the period up to 2011.

1.2   The primary purpose of this guidance is to provide a regional framework for the preparation of local authority development plans and, in London, for the Mayor's Spatial Development Strategy. Throughout this guidance 'South East' refers to the Greater London area and the areas covered by the shire county, unitary and district councils for Bedfordshire, Berkshire, Buckinghamshire, East Sussex, Essex, Hampshire, Hertfordshire, the Isle of Wight, Kent, Oxfordshire, Surrey and West Sussex.

1.3   The other purpose of this guidance is to provide the spatial framework for other strategies and programmes. These include the preparation of local transport plans by local authorities, the regional strategies of the South East of England Development Agency (SEEDA) and East of England Development Agency (EEDA), and the strategies prepared by the Mayor of London including those for economic development and transport.

1.4   This guidance takes account of Government policies as set out in Planning Policy Guidance Notes (PPGs), Minerals Planning Guidance Notes (MPGs), circulars and other Government statements including White Papers. A list is included in the Annex and includes the new PPG11 (*Regional Planning*) published in October 2000. This RPG should be read in conjunction with the more detailed existing guidance contained in:

- *Thames Gateway Planning Framework* (RPG9a) issued in 1995;

- *Strategic Guidance for London Planning Authorities* (RPG3) issued in 1996 (to be superseded by the Mayor's *Spatial Development Strategy*); and

- *Strategic Planning Guidance for the River Thames* (RPG3b/9b) issued in 1997.

1.5   All parts of this guidance must be taken into account by local planning authorities in preparing their development plans and may be material to decisions on individual planning applications and appeals.

Preparation of Regional Planning Guidance

1.6   SERPLAN issued *A Sustainable Development Strategy for the South East* for consultation as Draft RPG9 in December 1998. This was the subject of a Public Examination held by an independent Panel, whose report was published in October 1999. After due consideration of the Panel's recommendations as well as all the representations made on the Draft RPG, the Secretary of State issued his *Proposed Changes to Draft RPG9* and *Reasons for the Proposed Changes* in March 2000. These were the subject of public consultation over a twelve week period, as a result of which the Secretary of State made further changes which are incorporated in this final guidance.

1.7   The process of preparation of this guidance by SERPLAN began prior to the publication of draft Planning Policy Guidance on Regional Planning, Draft PPG11 *(Regional Planning)* in February 1999. As a result, this guidance, in its present form, does not fully accord with the advice in PPG11 on the scope and format of RPG. In particular, it is insufficiently regionally specific in places and therefore resorts to references to national policy. In order to develop regional policy in a number of aspects, further work will be required as part of the updating and review process. The Secretary of State expects early reviews of this RPG, with advice from the new regional planning bodies, particularly in respect of:

- Retail strategy (chapter 5);

- Tourism, including links with sport, recreation and cultural facilities (chapter 7);

- Housing provision and distribution in the light of monitoring and the results of urban capacity studies and potential growth area studies (chapter 8);

- Regional transport strategy (chapter 9);

- Waste and renewable energy (chapter 10);

- Minerals (chapter 11); and

- Monitoring (chapter 13).

Regional Planning Bodies and the Mayor of London

1.8   Throughout this guidance reference is made to 'Regional Planning Bodies and the Mayor of London'. These bodies have responsibility for implementation, monitoring and review of this guidance. They include SERPLAN who are the existing Regional Planning Body, the new Mayor of London and the organisations which will assume responsibility for regional planning in the Government Office regions for the South East and East of England once SERPLAN is wound up in March 2001. Bedfordshire, Essex and Hertfordshire will be joined with Cambridgeshire, Norfolk and Suffolk in a new East of England regional planning body, and the South East of England Regional Assembly will become the new regional planning body for the Government Office South East region.

1.9   The Mayor of London is preparing a Spatial Development Strategy for London. Future reviews of RPG for the Eastern and South East regions are to be based on Government Office boundaries. However, given the economic, transportation and social interdependence of London and the wider South East Region, pan-regional co-ordination arrangements have been agreed between the Greater London Authority and the new regional planning bodies for the South East and East of England regions.

Chapter 2

Context

2.1   With around 18.1 million people the South East has the largest regional population in the UK. At its heart lies London, a world city with a population of some 7 million. Surrounding the capital, the Rest of the South East (ROSE) contains a number of large urban areas and many small to medium sized towns. These settlements together account for almost 11% of the land area of ROSE. The economy in the South East has gradually recovered from the recession of the early 1990s, with London again prospering as a major European and World City.

2.2   The Region is endowed with a high quality environment, which makes the area an attractive place to live and work. Much of the ROSE countryside is subject to major environmental, cultural and planning designations. For example, there are a number of World Heritage Sites and other heritage features. Outside the urban areas, over 50% of all the land is covered by national or international designations including 24% by Green Belts. Together with strategic and local level designations of land, over 80% of the Region's non urban land in ROSE is subject to one or more policy designations or constraints.

2.3   The South East is a gateway to the rest of the United Kingdom, with transport infrastructure of national and international importance. This includes six major international airports, five international railway stations, six major ports as well as extensive railway and motorway networks. The opening of the Channel Tunnel and cheaper air fares have helped to reinforce the Region's links with neighbouring European countries and stronger economic relationships continue to develop.

2.4   Since publication of the last Regional Planning Guidance in 1994, there have been many developments in the international and national context as well as progress made in implementing the regional strategy. A number of these factors are highlighted in this chapter and they provide the context within which this guidance was formulated.

Sustainable Development

2.5   There is a growing understanding that economic, social and environmental issues are inextricably linked. While there continues to be a need for development, it is now recognised that future development cannot simply follow the models of the past. The Government has signed up to a number of international agreements, particularly on climate change and biodiversity, and these commitments are being translated into actions through national and local programmes. Furthermore, since the publication of RPG9 (1994), national planning guidance has been providing more rigorous guidance on sustainable development. In particular, there is now an emphasis on concentrating development in places well served by public transport, especially town centres, within urban areas and on previously developed sites, before considering the option of developing on greenfield sites.

Regionalisation

2.6 Since the last review, the regional administrative and representative infrastructure has been strengthened in the UK. RPG9 (1994) announced the establishment of the Integrated Regional Government Offices, which became known as the Government Offices. Subsequently, in April 1999, the Government established Regional Development Agencies in each English region including the South East of England Development Agency (SEEDA) and East of England Development Agency (EEDA). They were tasked to produce regional economic strategies, the first of which they produced in October 1999.

2.7 Regional Chambers, comprising local authorities and other regional partners, were set up during 1999. These include the South East of England Regional Assembly and East of England Regional Assembly. They are involved in preparing the regional sustainable development frameworks requested by Government. The Greater London Authority has been established with a Mayor of London and will publish a Spatial Development Strategy. The Mayor will also be responsible for publishing a series of other strategies including a transport strategy and an economic development strategy to be prepared by the London Development Agency.

2.8 Increasingly Government agencies, economic partnerships, networks of voluntary sector organisations, regional cultural consortia and others are also being organised along the same boundaries as the Government Offices, Regional Development Agencies and Regional Chambers.

European Perspective

2.9 A greater emphasis on regional planning has also emerged at the European level. The *European Spatial Development Perspective* (ESDP, 1999) sets the European framework for economic and social cohesion, sustainable development and balanced competitiveness of the European territory. It points to the need to achieve a more balanced urban system, a stronger relationship between urban and rural areas, integrated transport and communications, and intelligent management of natural and cultural heritage. The ESDP actively promotes co-operation between European regions and member states, for example through projects funded under the Interreg programmes. These have also assisted transnational programmes between parts of the South East Region and neighbouring European regions.

2.10 Of all the European Union programmes, in financial terms, the budget for the European Common Agricultural Policy (CAP) is likely to have the most extensive influence on spatial development in the Region through its implications for agricultural activity and land management. In the light of changes in agriculture, the European Union Rural Development Regulation is intended to assist rural diversification and shift some of the budgetary emphasis from production to environmental conservation.

2.11 European regional and social policy are mainly implemented by means of the European Structural Funds. These assist targeted parts of the South East as well as contribute to training measures. Other European programmes also target particular local areas or sectors.

2.12 European legislation continues to have direct and indirect implications for the South East Region. For example, additional areas of the South East are being designated under the European Habitats Directive. Another important piece of legislation is the European Landfill Directive, which will have implications for the cost of landfill and increase the incentive for regional partners to develop additional waste treatment facilities.

International and Global Developments

2.13   The South East, with the world city of London at its centre, is competing on the international stage and will be influenced by international and global events and decision-making. It is not possible to predict all the factors which will have direct and indirect impacts on the South East. However, it is possible to highlight some of the financial and institutional developments which should be monitored in terms of their impacts on the Region. Key developments within Europe include the enlargement of the European Union and the introduction of European Monetary Union which could affect the role of London as an international financial centre.

2.14   Key global developments include the liberalisation of international trade which is affecting, for example, traditional sectors such as agriculture and manufacturing. Furthermore, electronic forms of commercial transaction (e-commerce) are increasingly important. The total impact of e-commerce on employment is unclear. It may remove jobs in intermediary organisations whose perceived added value is undermined. At the same time it is likely to lead to jobs both in new industries like information brokerage and in established industries such as distribution and logistics.

Climate Change

2.15   In physical terms, the rate of climate change is now recognised as a significant global threat to the current way of life. Even with the achievement of internationally agreed targets to reduce greenhouse gas emissions, climate change is inevitable and is likely to have considerable impacts. The South East Region is particularly sensitive to the effects of climate change. Over the past century average temperature has risen by 0.5°C and summer rainfall has decreased. Around the Region's coastline the sea-level is rising, threatening important coastal habitats and increasing the risk of flooding. At the same time, a land tilt of about 6 millimetres a year in the South East, will also influence the relative rise in sea-level. Generally, greater climate changes are predicted whereby it will be warmer all year round, winters will be wetter and summers much drier. Weather extremes – such as the storms that caused the great floods on the eastern coastline in 1953, the storm of 1987 and the unusually warm summer of 1995 - may occur more frequently in the 21st century.

2.16   *Rising to the Challenge*, a study on the impacts of climate change in the South East in the 21st Century, indicated that coastal features such as Hurst Castle, land in the Solent and East Head at the mouth of Chichester Harbour risk being lost in more frequent coastal storms. Furthermore, ports are likely to be affected by more frequent storms and winds. Without adaptation, water shortages could be commonplace every summer and flooding in winters could make flood plains more hazardous places to live. Greater attention needs to be given to planning new developments so as to avoid areas with a tendency to flood and to take account of the availability of water resources. Climate change could also have other implications, for example, the need to anticipate deterioration of built structures, to avoid disruption to transport and power supplies or changes in cropping patterns – including the crops needed for renewable energy – and the associated development required for processing and storage.

RPG9 (1994) and the Need for Review

2.17   The strategy set out in RPG9 (1994) aimed to achieve a shift in the balance between the west and east of the Region. At the start of this millennium, London remains the major influence on the economy of the South East and the relationship between ROSE and London continues to be strong. Some regeneration and redevelopment is being achieved within the Thames Gateway, but progress has been slower than expected and the strategy advocated in RPG9 (1994) has yet to be realised. Decentralisation pressures are once again increasing in the Region and major urban areas, including much of the Thames Gateway, continue to show the highest rates of unemployment, with some of the inner London boroughs being among the most deprived in the UK.

2.18   Economic change has also had an impact on rural areas in the South East with a decline in traditional employment such as agriculture, defence industries and extractive industry, but a growth in small scale manufacturing and leisure and tourism. Overall in the South East, costs relative to the rest of the UK have risen and although the South East's Gross Domestic Product (GDP) per capita is the highest of any of the UK regions, it still trails behind a number of other European regions.

2.19   The activities of the Region's population and workforce inevitably lead to pressures being placed on the Region's environment and natural resources, its water, air and land. The demand for water arising from the Region's large population, within one of the driest regions in the country, is a cause for concern. Another threat to the Region's long term prosperity is widespread congestion owing to increasingly complex and lengthy commuting journeys and the growth in other types of journeys such as school trips. Increasing car usage is leading to major congestion and pollution problems.

2.20   It is accepted that a strategy is now required which is more sensitive to the diversity within the Region and which sets the direction for future changes. The process of long term change is gradual. The environment, society and economy of the South East twenty years hence will be shaped by decisions made now. It is important that regional policies respond not only to short term requirements, but also to a longer term view of the future of the Region.

Chapter 3

Vision and Key Development Principles

Vision

3.1 This guidance has a vision of encouraging economic success throughout the Region, ensuring a higher quality of environment with management of natural resources, opportunity and equity for the Region's population, and a more sustainable pattern of development. The focus is on enabling urban renaissance, promoting regeneration and renewal, concentrating development in urban areas, promoting a prosperous and multi-purpose countryside and promoting wider choice in travel options, thereby reducing the reliance on the private car.

3.2 The four objectives for sustainable development, as set out in the *Strategy for Sustainable Development in the UK*, are:

   a   Social progress which recognises the needs of everyone;

   b   Effective protection of the environment;

   c   Prudent use of natural resources; and

   d   Maintenance of high and stable levels of economic growth and employment.

3.3 The complex inter-relationships exhibited in the South East, particularly with London and the pressure on resources, suggest that it is only through the rigorous application of sustainable development principles that the economic success of the Region can be secured, whilst at the same time maintaining its environmental and cultural attractiveness and fostering social inclusion. Consideration of the sustainable development objectives means that changes have to be made in the way in which development proceeds in the future. These need to be incorporated in development plans and in the strategies of other organisations in order to ensure the Region's success.

Key Development Principles

3.4 It will be important to build on the growing consensus among the key stakeholders in the Region, seeking to redefine the pattern of development in the Region, and to ensure its continued environmental, economic and social health.

3.5 The main principles that should govern the continuing development of the Region are:

   1   Urban areas should become the main focus for development through making them more attractive, accessible and better able to attract investment;

   2   Greenfield development (namely, on previously undeveloped land) should normally take place only after other alternatives have been considered, and should have regard to the full social, environmental and transport costs of location;

3   The pattern of development should be less dispersed with more sustainable patterns of activity, allowing home, work, leisure, green spaces, cultural facilities and community services to be in closer proximity;

4   London's World City role and the South East's international connections should be developed as a basis for the enhancement of the Region's attractiveness in Europe and the world;

5   Economic opportunities should be increased by raising skills levels and reducing the disparities between different parts of the Region. In particular, by positive investment strategies for the Thames Gateway and Priority Areas for Economic Regeneration to improve the performance of poorer parts of the Region and by managing the localised impacts of development in economically buoyant areas;

6   Sufficient housing, and in particular affordable housing, should be provided for all who need to live and work in the Region, to encourage social inclusion and avoid pressure for housing in adjoining regions;

7   The development of housing should be more sustainable, providing a better mix of sizes, types and tenures, having regard to the structure of households and people's ability to access homes and jobs;

8   Development should be located and designed to enable more sustainable use of the Region's natural resources, in the supply of food, water, energy, minerals and timber, in the effective management of waste, the promotion of renewable energy sources and to assist in reducing pollution of air, land and water;

9   There should be continued protection and enhancement of the Region's biodiversity, internationally and nationally important nature conservation areas, and enhancement of its landscape and built and historic heritage;

10   The life of the countryside and rural communities should be sustained through economic diversification which respects the character of different parts of the Region and enables sustainable agriculture and forestry;

11   Access to jobs, services, leisure and cultural facilities should be less dependent on longer distance movement and there should be increased ability to meet normal travel needs through safe walking, cycling and public transport with reduced reliance on the car; and

12   Transport investment should support the spatial strategy, maintaining the existing network, enhancing access as part of more concentrated forms of development, overcoming bottlenecks and supporting higher capacity and less polluting modes of transport.

Urban Renaissance and Concentrating Development

3.6   A key feature of the strategy set out in this guidance is the concentration of development in urban areas. This concentration of development needs to be accompanied by action to secure a true urban renaissance in all the Region's urban areas, including suburban areas. The policies in subsequent chapters aim to secure both a concentration of development and an urban renaissance.

3.7   Design and management of the physical environment in urban areas, alongside policies to foster social inclusion and economic success, will be crucial to achieving a step change in the quality of urban life, making the towns and cities of the South East more attractive places in which to live, work and engage in cultural and leisure activity, and to invest. Local authorities will need to work with a wide variety of partners and local communities in order to achieve this renaissance. Such a co-ordinated approach will also be applicable to the smaller market towns throughout the Region which play an important role as service providers for their rural hinterlands.

Economy in the Use of Land

3.8   Rising incomes are likely to result in increasing demands for all goods and services, including land for living, working and for leisure. However, such demands cannot be met by present patterns of development and movement unless the quality of the environment is to suffer and social inequity to result. Large parts of the Region contain areas of significant environmental quality and there are many features of heritage or cultural value. These all contribute to the international attractiveness of the Region on which its future wellbeing is likely to depend.

3.9   Better use therefore needs to be made of land in the South East. This guidance sets a clear policy framework within which local authorities should assess the capacity of their urban areas for development. Better use then needs to be made of all the available urban land, including previously developed land. This is likely to require the design of more varied forms of development, integrating different uses including open space in urban areas. Designated Green Belts will continue their long term strategic role in shaping urban form and maintaining openness around and between urban areas.

3.10   National policies require a sequential approach to development. This in turn requires cross-boundary collaboration between local authorities to identify sufficient suitable locations for development. Town centres should be the normal focus of retailing and services requiring accessibility by large numbers of people. Industry and business development should be sustainable, both in the ease of access by walking, cycling and public transport, and in the layout and design of development. The amounts of land used for car parking should be minimised. The growing number of single person and small households, elderly households and those requiring special needs should be provided for.

3.11   This provides an opportunity to diversify the mix of the dwelling stock, with the provision of more smaller units, and opportunities to provide new forms of dwellings suitable for those who would prefer to share accommodation or communal services. Family dwellings will continue to be needed, but not as exclusively as in the past, and layouts must allow safe and secure streets and spaces for children. In particular, peripheral estates of poor layout which are remote from local and town services, and which depend on cars, must be avoided.

Integrating Land Use and Transport

3.12   In order to meet the sustainable development objectives for the Region, transport investment will need to be directed to support the urban renaissance. Transport exerts an important influence on the region, by facilitating movement, and by physically taking up space, especially for the parking and movement of cars. Congestion in parts of the Region is at a level that will provide a constraint on growth unless changes are made to the way people and goods travel.

3.13   Transport and land use will need to be more closely integrated, through development plans, local transport plans and through the strategies of key players in the Region. For the Region to function successfully in the future and to create safer and more sustainable places, greater reliance will need to be placed on walking, cycling and public transport, together with a recognition of the role that new technology can play in reducing the need to travel. This will require innovative solutions, particularly in rural areas, given the smaller populations and greater distances involved in journeys in rural areas.

3.14   Policies in the Regional Transport Strategy (see chapter 9) cover both intra-urban and inter-urban transport needs. There will be opportunities in urban areas and in transport corridors to secure the necessary modal shift that will allow greater interaction and accessibility without excessive use of land and the continued dispersal of activities. The multi-modal studies will assist in defining needs in the future, and this guidance will need early review to provide a full Regional Transport Strategy as a basis for future local transport plans.

Rural Development

3.15   The environmental quality and variety of the countryside are among the defining characteristics of the South East. A significant area of the countryside is recognised to be of international and national importance in terms of its nature conservation, landscape and cultural value. However, little of the South East's countryside is far from a town or city and most of the Region's population is employed in the urban-based economy. Rural areas are, therefore, subject to strong development and recreational pressure. Furthermore, despite the relative prosperity of the Region, significant areas of deprivation also exist in rural areas, the result of poor accessibility and decline in traditional rural based activities including agriculture. The continuing viability of many rural enterprises, local community services and facilities is of increasing concern.

3.16   The essence of the strategy for rural areas seeks to combine:

- securing a multi-purpose countryside, protecting it from inappropriate development and enhancing its natural and cultural resources; with

- supporting targeted measures to help sustain the economic and social vitality of rural communities.

Government has produced the *England Rural Development Plan* outlining its approach to addressing issues facing rural areas. This guidance emphasises that a vital and multi-purpose countryside requires innovative approaches to the provision of local housing, employment, leisure, transport and community facilities to help enhance social inclusion whilst reducing the need to travel long distances. The role of market towns in providing a focus for economic development, local services, transport links and cultural activity in rural areas, is also highlighted. Integrated packages of policies are required at a local level in order to assist in balancing the need for environmental protection with measures needed to sustain and enhance the economic and social viability of rural communities.

Chapter 4

Core Strategy for the Region

4.1 The economic and geographic structure of the South East is complex and it is not possible to subdivide it into rigid sub areas. There is, however, an underlying spatial pattern and structure to its economic activity and opportunities. This chapter sets out the key components of the spatial structure of the Region. It has regard to the structure as set out in the previous RPG9 (1994), although some of the details have changed in the light of altered circumstances and policy. This chapter should be read together with Map 2.

The Region in Europe and the UK

4.2 The South East Region is the main gateway between the UK and neighbouring European countries for business, trade and many other aspects of national life. This guidance recognises that the Region is important as a zone of communication, and every effort should be made to ensure the co-ordination of different modes of transport and to have regard to the international role of gateways in the Region. Furthermore, the Region's proximity to the northern regions of France, Belgium and the Netherlands also implies that greater attention be paid to the relationships between London, the capital cities of Paris, Brussels and Amsterdam and their respective hinterlands. Ongoing work is required by regional partners to reflect the cross-Channel interrelationships and the European spatial development agenda. This includes issues of common interest such as coastal management and port development on both sides of the Channel. Regional partners could pursue this work by building upon existing initiatives, for example, joint planning work between Kent County Council and the Nord/Pas de Calais Region.

4.3 The relationships across regional boundaries within the UK are also increasingly important. For example, the movement of population between ROSE and neighbouring UK regions. This guidance recognises the importance of such linkages and the need to co-operate with the neighbouring UK regions of the South West, East Midlands and West Midlands. In future, the Regional Planning Bodies for the South East and East of England and the Mayor for London will need to take particular care in ensuring that arrangements are put in place to ensure that plans for the three areas are co-ordinated, given the complex inter-relationships between London and its neighbouring regions. A protocol for future pan-regional arrangements has been drawn up by the new Regional Planning Bodies and the Mayor for London. Both inter-regional and intra-regional links are likely to become more important and should be reflected in future reviews of this guidance.

4.4 Within the Region local authorities will also need to collaborate with their neighbours. Some specific sub-regions where this is the case are identified in this guidance. Local authorities through the Regional Planning Bodies should explore further areas where networking and transnational co-operation could help to maximise the opportunities created by the proximity of continental Europe.

London

4.5   London is located at the heart of the South East Region and at the hub of national and international transport and communications networks. This guidance provides the context for the wide range of complex interdependent relationships that exist between London and its hinterland. Strategic planning policies for the capital which are set out separately in the Secretary of State's RPG3 *(Strategic Guidance for London Planning Authorities)* will be replaced by the Mayor of London's Spatial Development Strategy. Except where indicated in the text, this guidance does not replace or duplicate the policies set out in those documents, but it provides the wider regional framework within which the policies for London are set and should be considered. Circular 1/2000 *(Strategic Planning in London)* sets out the Mayor of London's role in representing London's planning interests in discussions about broader regional planning matters.

4.6   Future development in London should support and develop London's role as a world business and commercial centre and as a centre of international and national importance for retailing, tourism, education, heritage, culture and the arts. It should also maximise the advantages, for the Region as a whole, of proximity to London's national and international service economy and businesses, and to the range of other facilities it offers. Future development should support the regeneration in areas of deprivation in London having regard to the need to encourage sustainable development. The land use and transport planning policies in this guidance have an important role to play in meeting these objectives. The level and distribution of provision for new housing and employment uses across the Region as a whole are important elements in securing sustainable economic growth, social inclusion and improved quality of life for both London and ROSE. Transport policies play a crucial role in maintaining and developing efficient and sustainable public transport networks across the region, including supplying London with a significant proportion of its labour force. It is important to maintain London's attractiveness as a place to live and work and to avoid decentralisation of economic activity, skills and jobs from London, which would threaten its position as a world city, undermine regeneration initiatives and adversely affect the Region as a whole.

4.7   London will continue to offer a very sustainable location within the Region for business, retail and leisure development. It should also continue to maximise its contribution to the regional housing provision, consistent with maintaining and enhancing the quality of life in the capital, and through realistic assessments of capacity. A particular objective in meeting London's potential to accommodate growth will be to seek balanced and mixed development consistent with the objectives of urban renaissance and maintaining high levels of environmental quality. Previously developed land within London, its town centres and regeneration corridors all have an important role in accommodating growth consistent with sustainability principles.

4.8   The close interconnectivity between London and its hinterland should be reflected through common policy approaches where appropriate. This is particularly important in sub-regions and transport corridors which cross the London boundary, for example the Lea Valley, the Thames Valley and orbital routes around London. Chapters 9 and 12 provide examples of where these common approaches can be achieved.

Thames Gateway

4.9   The regeneration of the Thames Gateway is a regional and national priority. This guidance recognises the complexity of the area's structural problems but also emphasises the potential for Thames Gateway to make a vital and major contribution to the growth of the regional economy and the enhancement of its environment. Extensive areas of derelict land, the availability of surplus labour and the proximity to Central London, international transport hubs and continental Europe are some of the factors which combine to make this area a unique opportunity for the Region.

4.10 RPG9a *(Thames Gateway Planning Framework)*, together with RPG9b/3b *(Strategic Planning Guidance for the River Thames)*, contain strategic planning guidance for the sustainable development of the area and for the River Thames. The Secretary of State has decided to extend the boundary of the Thames Gateway eastwards within South Essex to include more of Thurrock, part of Basildon District (including Basildon New Town), the Boroughs of Castle Point and Southend-on-Sea and London Southend Airport which is largely in Rochford District. This reflects the advice from SERPLAN that the areas in South Essex have similar problems and opportunities as the rest of the Thames Gateway area and already have strong functional links with London.

4.11 This guidance does not replace or duplicate the policies set out in RPG9a, but provides the wider spatial framework for Thames Gateway. An early review of RPG9a is required. However, until RPG9a is updated, the principles it contains will also apply to the new parts of the Thames Gateway and should be reflected in the preparation of future development plans and planning applications.

4.12 The vision for the extended Thames Gateway is that of a strong and diverse sub-region. The opportunities presented by the area should be maximised to enable the Thames Gateway to compete effectively, offering a comprehensive transport system and a quality environment for new businesses and homes. A skilled workforce will be crucial to facilitate growth. Local communities should derive maximum benefit from regeneration opportunities. Development should reflect the importance of the River Thames estuary for biodiversity and recreation and also the associated habitats of international and national importance.

4.13 Implementation of RPG9a remains a priority. The Thames Gateway should continue to be the focus of public and private investment in regeneration and growth. Transport infrastructure is a significant component. In order to achieve this, the Regional Development Agencies, Mayor of London, Regional Chambers and Planning Bodies, the three Government Offices and the numerous local authorities will need to co-operate with other stakeholders in co-ordinating their efforts and programmes. The Government has established a new Strategic Partnership for this purpose, bringing these key bodies together to take forward the long term development and growth of the area, and is encouraging the development of effective delivery mechanisms.

Rest of the South East (ROSE)

4.14 Throughout the ROSE area development should be primarily concentrated within urban areas, in line with the principles set out in chapter 3. It should enable the renaissance of urban areas, the integration of transport, a multi-purpose countryside and the conservation of natural resources in the Region. However, the South East is a polycentric Region and outside of London and the Thames Gateway, ROSE covers a diversity of local economies. This guidance highlights different parts of ROSE which require particular policy approaches.

i Priority Areas for Economic Regeneration (PAERs)

4.15 The South East does not enjoy a uniformly prosperous economy and there are some substantial areas of deprivation as well as smaller pockets of deprivation in many otherwise prosperous towns. For example, the National Index of Multiple Deprivation (2000) ranks 191 wards in 40 districts of the South East among the worst decile of deprived wards in the UK. A sustainable development strategy must tackle such deprivation, both because achieving social inclusion is a fundamental aspect of sustainable development and because making best use of the Region's resources, including land and people, will increase its overall economic performance and achieve a more equitable distribution of prosperity around the Region.

4.16 Smaller pockets of deprivation will need to be tackled locally, but a number of areas of regional significance are identified in this guidance as Priority Areas for Economic Regeneration (PAERs). The criteria for designation include above average unemployment rates, high levels of social deprivation, low skill levels, dependence on declining industries, derelict urban fabric, peripherality and insularity. These areas need tailored regeneration strategies backed up by appropriate resources to address their problems and maximise their contribution to the social and economic well-being of the region.

4.17 The PAERs identified in this Guidance are: South Hampshire, Southampton and Portsmouth; the Isle of Wight; the Sussex Coastal Towns from Shoreham Harbour to Hastings; the former coalfields and coastal towns of East Kent; Harlow; East London and the Lower Lea Valley; Luton, Dunstable and Houghton Regis; and the Tendring Coast.

4.18 Each PAER has its own distinctive set of problems and will need individually tailored strategies. Chapter 12 gives further guidance on each PAER. Many are already designated as areas which qualify for regional, national or European funding programmes. It will be important for expenditure under such programmes to be co-ordinated with local spending programmes through partnership working, and for strategies to be locally designed. Strategies to tackle social exclusion should be based on communities' own assessment of their need and should encourage participation through Local Strategic Partnerships and other mechanisms. They should be inclusive in their implementation. Urban renaissance will be a key part of the strategy for most PAERs.

4.19 Planning policies have an important role to play in implementing PAER strategies, through policies on the designation of employment sites, re-use of brownfield land, transport access, and urban renewal and intensification.

ii Western Policy Area

4.20 The Western Policy Area is an area to the west and south of London, ranging broadly from the M1 and Watford in the north, Reading in the west and Gatwick to the south. It covers parts of Berkshire, Buckinghamshire, Oxfordshire, Hampshire and Surrey together with areas around Heathrow and Gatwick airports. The area as a whole is economically very buoyant and characterised by pressures and constraints which can be measured, in particular with respect to the tightness in the labour market, housing and property markets and transport issues.

4.21 The success of the area has been based on an economic structure which has a strong representation in a range of high-tech industries and a clustering of important economic activities. These businesses add value to the economy and are important in sustaining the competitiveness of the economy generally. There are, however, local pockets of deprivation within this otherwise buoyant area.

4.22 Economic development strategies for this area should build on its economic strengths, particularly the high skill levels and knowledge base, to ensure that the economy continues to grow in a sustainable way with the minimum additional pressure on limited labour or land resources. Local planning authorities, with the support of SEEDA, face the challenge of enabling continued economic prosperity in this area while discouraging new development of a type which would be unsustainable. The positive tackling of 'hotspots' or localised areas with problems will be particularly important and further guidance is included in chapter 7.

4.23 Local authorities, economic partnerships, business support organisations, the Regional Development Agencies and others should work together to adopt an approach which both understands and recognises the area's economic strengths and the importance of maintaining an environment that is attractive to investment in this area. Developers are able to contribute to costs of providing required physical and community infrastructure through the use of section 106 agreements between local authorities and developers.

iii Potential Growth Areas

4.24 Chapter 3 explains that concentration of development is key to a sustainable development strategy for the Region. This applies throughout the Region and implies that urban areas will be the focus for new development. In the longer term there may be a need for additional urban growth areas to be identified as a way of concentrating growth in a sustainable and planned way. At this stage two potential growth areas are identified at Milton Keynes and Ashford. In addition, a study is proposed to investigate the need for development and the options for accommodating it in the London-Stansted-Cambridge area. A strategy for the London-Stansted-Cambridge sub-region will need to draw upon the study and be taken forward in the London Spatial Development Strategy and future regional planning guidance for the East of England.

4.25 Such growth areas will need to take a comprehensive plan-led approach to development, ensuring jobs and homes increase in parallel and that the necessary physical and community infrastructure is provided at the required time to create sustainable communities. Efficient use of land to concentrate development will be particularly important so that it can be effectively served by public transport as well as encourage walking and cycling. Local authorities will need to work closely with neighbouring authorities where a growth area crosses administrative boundaries or could have impacts in neighbouring authorities.

Chapter 5

Quality of Life in Town and Country

5.1   A good quality of life means ensuring that the economy, society and the environment develop in harmony. The vision for the South East, as set out in chapter 3 of this guidance, is to bring about an urban renaissance in order to improve the quality of life for those in urban areas and to protect the countryside. Urban renaissance is about creating the quality of life that makes urban living desirable, making better use of land and energy and increasing the sense of community in urban areas throughout the South East.

5.2   This chapter emphasises the need to integrate spatial development with the management of resources as well as the need for regional partners to co-operate in taking a holistic approach to urban and rural areas. Ultimately, urban renaissance and sustainable rural areas will be achieved only if rooted in local ownership. The renewal and long term management of urban and rural neighbourhoods requires local authorities to take a lead by developing a strategic vision for the future of each urban and rural area in the Region, and by encouraging a co-ordinated approach to realising that vision. Local communities must be involved in developing this vision and in developing their own local agendas. Community strategies and local strategic partnerships can play useful roles in this process. The development of local policies, support for local services and the enhancement of cultural provision and activity can help to reinforce a sense of place to the local area, strengthen communities and reduce the need to travel.

Box 1 - Central Principles of Urban Renaissance as Formulated by the Urban Task Force

The sustained success of urban areas will be predicated upon five central principles:

- achieving design excellence;
- creating economic strength;
- taking environmental responsibility;
- investing in urban government; and
- prioritising social well-being

Source: Towards an Urban Renaissance, Final report of the Urban Task Force chaired by Lord Rogers of Riverside, 1999.

Urban Renaissance and Concentrating Development

5.3   Urban areas in the South East range from London, the capital city with a population of some 7 million, to small and historic towns. There are a number of large urban concentrations outside of London such as Southampton and Portsmouth. The Thames Gateway area itself comprises part of east London and a series of large and medium sized towns. There is scope for increasing the linkages between towns such that they form networks of urban areas and thus enhance choice for local residents in accessing employment and services.

5.4 Many towns and cities have expanded during the past decades and most people now live in suburban areas. Future development is to be accommodated within all parts of the urban areas of the South East, both within central areas and the suburbs, in order to make better use of land. Intensifying the use of urban areas offers many benefits in terms of maximising the viability of existing infrastructure and service provision at the same time as protecting the countryside of the South East. It can help to enhance the viability of public transport infrastructure through the increase of populations within catchments served by rail and bus services. Potential benefits in terms of sustaining established service provision range from community services such as education, health, social and cultural facilities, to water and energy supply.

Policy Q1

Urban areas should be the prime focus for new development and for redevelopment.

a   Development plans should:

    i   concentrate development within the Region's urban areas and seek to achieve at least 60% of all new development in ROSE on previously developed land and through conversions of existing buildings;

    ii   ensure that new developments in and around urban areas are well designed and consistent with the overall strategy for urban renaissance and sustainable development;

    iii   use growth opportunities to restructure existing urban areas by encouraging development in and around existing centres and promoting local neighbourhood centres as places where people can go for day-to-day shopping and other services;

    iv   have regard to advice in PPG3 *(Housing)* on developing outside urban areas; and

    v   where greenfield land is to be used for development as part of a wider land use strategy, ensure that the form of development is consistent with the overall strategy for urban renaissance and sustainable development, making the best use land and access to public transport infrastructure and services.

b   In addition local authorities should:

    i   use the process of undertaking urban capacity studies to identify which sites may also be suitable for uses other than housing. Further reference to urban capacity studies is included in chapter 8 of this guidance and PPG3 *(Housing)*; and

    ii   make use of compulsory purchase orders to assist in the assembly of urban sites, including town centre sites, for redevelopment for a mix of uses. The Government has commissioned the preparation of a procedure manual to assist authorities, and is considering further improvements to the compulsory purchase regime.

Form and Design of Urban Development

5.5 Focusing development within urban areas will require careful attention to the form and design of development. In the South East the design of redevelopment of parts of urban areas is as important as the location and design of new development. Increasingly creative solutions are being found which:

- maximise the opportunities for renewal;

- strive for a greater mix of building types, land uses and tenures; and

- seek to optimise development density in proximity to public transport hubs in and around existing centres and within a network of multi-functional open spaces.

Guidance on the location and design of development is contained in Planning Policy Guidance notes (PPGs) including PPG1 *(General Policy and Principles)*, PPG3 *(Housing)*, PPG6 *(Town Centres and Retail Developments)*, PPG7 *(The Countryside – Environmental Quality and Economic and Social Development)* and Draft PPG13 *(Transport)*.

5.6   Mixing different land uses throughout cities or towns can serve to strengthen social integration and civic life. PPG1 *(General Policy and Principles)* and PPG6 *(Town Centres and Retail Developments)* advise on the advantages of mixed use. Such forms of development are also important in suburbs where a high quality living environment can be provided with a mix of uses and good public transport connections to town or city centres. Even in recently developed suburbs it is possible to make small scale improvements that benefit the way in which suburbs function; for example, by improving townscape and public spaces and by focussing facilities that meet day-to-day needs in local neighbourhood centres.

5.7   Whether in existing urban areas, including suburban areas, or in urban extensions or new settlements, 'urban villages' are a form of urban development that can meet many of the demands of modern living and enhance quality of life. The term is used to describe mixed-use areas where people can live, work and meet their everyday shopping and lifestyle needs. They can provide a range of housing choices to accommodate changing lifestyles, ensure safe streets to encourage walking and cycling and good access to public transport, incorporate support for local businesses and local jobs, and encourage a stronger sense of community. In doing so, urban villages promote a more sustainable form of urban development, delivering a range of improved environmental and social outcomes and improving the quality of urban life through building better neighbourhoods.

5.8   In achieving design excellence, there is a need to embrace innovation, for example, in terms of designing energy efficient buildings or organising car-free neighbourhoods. At the same time, the best of the Region's cultural and natural heritage needs to be protected and preserved. The future development of urban neighbourhoods must therefore be based on an understanding of their historic character, preserving and adapting historic buildings to accommodate new uses and provide a focus for urban communities and enhancing the urban rivers, parks and other green spaces. Further guidance is provided in PPG15 *(Planning and the Historic Environment)*.

5.9   The design of individual developments will be a major influence on the extent to which they are sustainable. Aspects of sustainable design include:

• use of waste prevention and minimisation techniques;

• installation of pollution abatement technology to reduce emissions to air and water;

• control measures for surface water drainage as close to its source as possible;

• building design which facilitate the use of renewable energy;

• energy efficient installations, including passive solar design for buildings and improved insulation;

• water efficient installations, including the use of grey water systems;

• use of renewable and recycled materials during construction and design to facilitate recycling systems, including combined heat and power and community heating schemes; and

• use of 'soft' construction and maintenance techniques harnessing natural processes.

Such measures are cited, for example, in chapter 10 of this guidance.

5.10   The provision of a more sustainable pattern of development, reconciling the need for dwellings in the South East whilst avoiding unnecessary encroachment into the countryside will only be possible where local authorities encourage better design and resist car dependent forms of development. In general, densities in ROSE have been some of the lowest in the country, increasing the amount of greenfields taken for new development. There is, therefore, considerable scope within the South East for accommodating homes in ways which save land and create viable catchments for local services and public transport.

Box 2 - Approach and Principles of Sustainable Residential Quality (SRQ) in London and the South East (Studies by Llewelyn-Davies)

The central question that the SRQ study tries to answer is: How can additional new dwellings be accommodated so as to maximise their contribution to improving the quality of urban life and to fostering new development?

The SRQ work is underpinned by five main themes:

- taking a positive view: urban capacity is an opportunity not a threat. Using previously used land sensitively can help to rebuild and integrate towns in ways that encourage more activity and life without leading to 'town cramming';

- relating housing potential to accessibility to public transport and local facilities: SRQ focuses on potential in areas within a ten minute walk of centres (termed the 'ped-shed'). In these areas residents can readily access good services, jobs and public transport on foot or by bike;

- taking a long term and imaginative view: the study looked beyond sites currently vacant to consider those that may be suitable for housing in the future. It is vital to look beyond today's sites and explore future potential in order to indicate the true extent of housing that could be realised;

- using a design-led approach: the study explores a set of different design options for each of the sites. This demonstrates what can be achieved by varying assumptions about dwelling mix, density and car parking provision, whilst maintaining a high quality of amenity; and

- SRQ raises questions about the context within which planning operates. For example, Neighbourhood Car Sharing Schemes could be adopted and 'community chests' could be used to fund and maintain local facilities.

Source: Sustainable Residential Quality – New Approaches to Urban Living (LPAC, 1997); Sustainable Residential Quality in the South East (GOSE, 1998)

Policy Q2

The quality of life in urban areas, including suburban areas, should be raised through significant improvement to the urban environment, making urban areas more attractive places in which to live, work, shop, spend leisure time and invest, thus helping to counter trends to more dispersed patterns of residence and travel.

a   Development plans should:

   i   set out an overall strategy for enhancing the quality of life in each urban area which reflects a vision developed in consultation with local communities;

   ii   encourage mixed use developments, for example by identifying suitable opportunities for urban villages;

   iii include proposals for local areas, including suburban neighbourhoods, which improve the integration between different land uses including local services, and enhance the viability of different modes of travel including walking, cycling and public transport;

iv identify key sites for which design solutions will need to be developed;

v make optimum use of existing buildings and infrastructure, especially protecting those of historic and cultural value;

vi utilise the opportunities for regeneration which may be created by new development;

vii maximise the positive contribution which trees, other planting and open spaces can make to urban areas in terms of their recreational, nature conservation and wider environmental and social benefits; and

viii promote design and layout solutions relevant to particular sites and their context, which take account of public health, crime prevention and community safety issues, and which build upon local distinctiveness.

b In addition:

i urban capacity studies will assist in identifying sites with scope for redevelopment;

ii site specific development briefs can guide landowners and developers. In preparing such briefs or proposals, local authorities and potential developers need to take into account the context including strategies for open space provision, other land uses and services and access;

iii it is important to maximise the essential contribution which open spaces, green corridors and trees can make to urban and rural areas in terms of their benefits for wildlife habitats, recreational and cultural value and wider environmental and social benefits. English Nature can advise on targets for accessible natural greenspace provision;

iv through the preparation of Local Transport Plans, local authorities should consider the best ways to further promote the management of traffic to achieve a better urban environment, including measures which improve road safety, give priority to pedestrians, cyclists, buses and essential business users, increase parking restrictions and improve integration between modes. Further guidance is provided in the *Regional Transport Strategy* (see chapter 9);

v all strategies, particularly in deprived areas, should take into account health impact assessments and advice on public health in order to maximise the opportunities for tackling the root causes of ill health;

vi local authorities should work with English Heritage, the Regional Cultural Consortia and others in developing innovative strategies for the management of historic buildings and sites and other cultural attractions. New uses may need to be found for many such buildings and sites in order to secure their long term future; and

vii local authorities should take steps to ensure that crime prevention considerations are incorporated in the design of new development. Crime prevention is capable of being a material consideration when planning applications are being considered. As with other material considerations, the weight that is given to it will depend upon the individual circumstances of the proposal. Local planning authorities may refuse planning applications when, on the advice of the police, they have significant concerns about the implications of a proposal on community safety.

Policy Q3

Development should be carefully located and designed to make better use of land and create viable catchments for services and infrastructure. New development, in particular housing, should make more efficient use of land throughout the Region.

a   In preparing development plans outside London, local authorities should:

   i   avoid developments which make inefficient use of land (those of less than 30 dwellings per hectare net);

   ii encourage housing development which makes more efficient use of land (between 30 and 50 dwellings per hectare net); and

   iii seek greater intensity of development in places with good public transport accessibility, such as town, district and local centres or at major nodes along good quality public transport corridors and major cities.

b   Within London and many urban areas across ROSE, there are significant opportunities to provide high quality housing development in excess of 50 dwellings per hectare net. Local authorities should take a positive approach to developing proposals for these areas to assist in meeting housing need and improve the quality of the urban environment.

c   In addition, local authorities should:

   i   work closely with local communities and potential developers and use the preparation of site specific development briefs for housing or mixed development to guide developers;

   ii maximise opportunities for increasing housing provision as part of a mixed use development; and

   iii integrate such developments with the provision of facilities for walking and cycling and public transport.

Urban Fringe

5.11   It is important to ensure the attractiveness of the urban fringe, which is the intermediary area between the urban area and open countryside or the fringe of an adjoining urban area. The urban fringe includes green space. It can be characterised by downgraded and under used agricultural land and fragmented ownership, but can offer scope for positive environmental improvements. Where development has to take place outside urban areas, PPG3 *(Housing)* advises that planned extensions to existing urban areas are likely to prove the next most sustainable option after building on appropriate sites within urban areas. Some parts of the existing urban fringe will be more suitable than others for extensions to urban areas, for example, those areas which are accessible by public transport and make it possible to utilise existing physical and social infrastructure. The need for and location of urban extensions will be of concern, for example, in the Potential Growth Areas which are to be the subject of studies referred to in chapter 12 of this guidance. At the same time, positive open space management is required where the urban fringe is to be better defined. Chapter 6 of this guidance elaborates on the protection of the countryside, including land around urban areas, particularly Green Belts.

Policy Q4

Land in the urban fringe should be enhanced, effectively managed and appropriately used.

a   Development plans should:

   i   ensure enhancement and better management of the urban fringe, for example, through identification of areas of importance for nature conservation or recreation or of coherent areas suitable for the continuation of agricultural use; and

ii   select, only where required, suitable areas for urban extensions. The requirement for urban extensions will be based on the sequential approach set out in PPG3 *(Housing)* and will need to reflect guidance on the protection of Green Belt and other designated areas. In these circumstances, local authorities should select those areas which would make effective use of previously developed sites and buildings on the urban fringe, such as redundant hospital sites and former defence sites where such development would be sustainable and where it would enhance the conservation, landscape or amenity value of the site.

b   In addition, local authorities should continue to work with a number of partners including the private sector and agencies such as Groundwork Trust and county wildlife trusts in formulating and implementing strategies for urban fringe areas.

Ensuring Vitality and Viability of Town and Local Centres

5.12   Urban renaissance should incorporate mechanisms to revive town centres. Town centres have suffered from the last recession and from the diversion of investment to out-of-centre retail developments. To reverse this trend there is a need to focus retailing development in town centres and to avoid further development in out-of-centre locations. In this chapter 'town centre' is used to cover city and town centres.

Policy Q5

The Region's existing network of larger town centres should be the focus for major retail, leisure and office developments, to support an urban renaissance, promote social inclusion and encourage more sustainable patterns of development.

a   In monitoring and reviewing this guidance, Regional Planning Bodies should assess the need outside London for major new retail and leisure facilities or large-scale expansion of existing retail and leisure facilities of regional and sub-regional importance. Furthermore, they should identify which town centres outside of London should be the focus for major retail development. Until this guidance has been reviewed and decisions made on the location of major retail and leisure development, substantial expansion of retail and leisure development of regional and sub-regional importance is unlikely to be justified in out-of-town locations.

b   The preferred locations for major office developments should be town centres or sites near to major public transport interchanges, although town centres should generally be preferred. All office developments should be well served or capable of being well served by public transport.

c   In preparing development plans, local authorities should:

i   take account of any reviews carried out by Regional Planning Bodies which assess the need outside of London for new retail and leisure facilities or large-scale expansion of existing retail and leisure facilities of regional and sub-regional importance;

ii   assess the need for retail, leisure and office development in their area;

iii   identify which town and district centres should be the preferred locations for growth; and

iv   apply the sequential approach set out in PPG6 *(Town Centres and Retail Developments)* to identify sites for retail, leisure and office development. Local authorities should avoid extending existing edge-of-centre and out-of-centre development while more central options exist.

d   In addition:

   i   town and district centre improvement strategies and management schemes can assist in improving the vitality and viability of centres. They require a close partnership between retailers and other town centre interests including local authorities. Many towns are now actively engaged in such strategies, which can focus on physical improvements as well as identifying, assembling and marketing sites, or objectives such as finding alternative uses for upper storey premises in order to reduce the number of empty properties.

   ii Positive management strategies should be adopted to secure the vitality of local and neighbourhood centres. In developing such strategies it is helpful to review land use in central areas taking account of factors such as:

   - the planned distribution of housing and population and the forecast growth in expenditure;

   - the physical capacity of existing centres and the scope for expansion whilst respecting historic character and cultural value;

   - the performance of existing centres, the scope for regeneration and improvement and for absorbing additional expenditure within existing floorspace;

   - the potential impact on the vitality and viability of nearby major town centres;

   - the capacity of transport infrastructure, especially accessibility by passenger transport; and

   - minimising the aggregate need for shoppers to travel, especially by car.

Management and the Provision of Services

5.13   Effective management and maintenance of buildings, public spaces, landscape and infrastructure is important for the sustained success of urban areas including suburban areas, as is the provision of public services. These include waste collection, street cleaning, lighting, traffic control and policing, as well as the provision of healthcare and education.

5.14   Promoting the health and well-being of people in the South East is important to quality of life. The Government's White Paper *Saving Lives: Our Healthier Nation* recognises that health is affected by a range of factors including the provision of a safe, secure and sustainable environment, reducing pollution, adequate housing provision, access to leisure and recreation, reducing social exclusion and increasing employment opportunities. These factors are considered by subsequent chapters of this guidance. In respect of healthcare, the White Paper identifies four priority health areas: heart disease and strokes, accidents, cancer and mental health, and sets targets to reduce death and disability from these causes by 2010. It proposes a contract indicating how national, regional and local bodies and individuals can participate in achieving better health. In July 2000 the Government issued the *National Health Service (NHS)* Plan setting out sustained increases in investment to enable modernisation of the service.

5.15   Modernisation of the NHS is expected to deliver major structural changes in health services over a period of about ten years. In many places it is likely to include:

   - increasing concentration of hospital specialities in fewer, more specialised centres; and

   - increasing the scope of primary care, for example, to include more routine treatments.

New facilities will need to be developed or redeveloped wherever possible on sites that are well served by public transport and accessible on foot or by cycle, to ensure access for patients, staff and visitors. Partnerships between the NHS Executive, Health Authorities and local care providers, including local authorities, are developing Health Improvement Programmes (HIMPs) which set out the local contribution to achieving national targets and objectives, including the modernisation of the NHS.

5.16 In respect of education provision, the Government is committed to supporting life long learning. In *The Learning Age: A Renaissance for A New Britain* the Government emphasises the need to increase access for potential learners whether they are individuals or enterprises. It points to the opportunity for learning to take place in many different types of location, whether at home, at work, in local libraries or shopping centres as well as colleges and universities. A creative approach is needed to identifying and providing facilities for education and training and this requires co-operation between local authorities and education providers.

5.17 Rural communities must have access to services such as healthcare and schools and also cultural facilities, in order to thrive. In view of the distances involved and the smaller population catchments, it is essential for regional partners to continue to develop innovative solutions to ensure the provision of community services and public transport in rural areas.

5.18 Tackling all these issues requires a co-ordinated approach between various agencies and bodies at all levels. A number of towns in the South East have been evolving new forms of management for council estates and town centres. Further initiatives are required, particularly at the local level to ensure the long term management of neighbourhoods. Local authorities have been preparing Local Agenda 21 strategies which consider all aspects of sustainable development and more recently Government has placed a duty on local authorities to prepare community plans for their local areas.

Policy Q6

Health, education and other social considerations and infrastructure requirements need to be taken into account fully in development planning throughout the Region.

a   Development plans should:

   i   facilitate the reconfiguration and modernisation of health services, in accordance with sustainable development principles, informed by partnership working with Health Authorities and others on Health Improvement Programmes;

   ii   have regard to the impacts of proposed developments on health of local communities, taking advice from NHS Executive Regional Offices;

   iii   enable the varied provision of facilities for education and training;

   iv   facilitate provision of other facilities required by local communities, wherever possible maximising the potential of existing community buildings and their associated land; and

   v   facilitate the location of services in places which are accessible for clients and staff by public transport and wherever possible, on foot and by cycle.

b   In addition:

   i   partnership working is required between various agencies including local authorities, housing associations, service providers and the utilities such as water companies to ensure that infrastructure provision is adequate and maintained;

   ii   all organisations and individuals are involved in the ongoing maintenance of the urban fabric. This ranges from the private individual who is responsible for the state of repair of their home to major institutions such as the local authorities' responsibilities for street cleaning and waste collection;

iii   Local Agenda 21 strategies and community strategies can help in the formulation and integration of such measures. Furthermore, they can play an important part in stimulating local involvement in the preparation of other local strategies; and

iv   local authorities, services providers, key agencies and others throughout the Region can improve the local environment, public health and safety by a variety of measures including:

- improved housing conditions;

- management of local air and water quality;

- reducing incidents of noise pollution;

- restoring derelict and contaminated land;

- emphasising the health benefits of walking, cycling and other physical activity; and

- improving community and primary health care services.

Rural Development

5.19   The characteristics of rural areas in the South East vary throughout the Region. In some areas the wealth and proximity of urban areas has resulted in a range of threats and opportunities for rural areas, whereas other areas remain less accessible, leading to fewer job opportunities, problems of isolation and lower incomes. The assessment and delivery of rural policy requires a tailored and integrated approach that focuses on people as well as places, to help maintain and enhance the environment whilst encouraging the development of diverse and sustainable rural communities.

5.20   The economic base of rural areas in the South East has been undergoing significant change over recent years, resulting in particular in employment decline in agriculture and related industries. This, combined with problems of isolation and accessibility, has resulted in a need to create new jobs and enterprise within many rural areas, particularly those areas identified as Rural Priority Areas (formerly known as Rural Development Areas). At the same time, there is a greater awareness of the need to protect and improve the rural environment. The Region needs to grasp those opportunities which exist to promote sensitive economic activity in rural areas, utilising positively their many environmental advantages, whilst also improving the long term viability of local communities. The means of achieving these combined objectives vary from one area to another. For example, the approach in Green Belt areas (around London, Oxford and South Hampshire and South Bedfordshire) will inevitably differ from that taken in remoter countryside.

5.21   Throughout the Region the countryside should fulfil a range of needs including recreation, farming, forestry, military uses and the local economy, while safeguarding landscape and biodiversity. Enhancement of the rural environment requires active countryside management as well as the maintenance of existing rural resources. Further guidance is contained in PPG7 (*The Countryside - Environmental Quality and Economic and Social Development*). Furthermore, the tranquillity, quality and variety of the Region's countryside, including villages and country estates, provide a major leisure asset for both inhabitants and visitors. If managed appropriately, both formal and informal leisure and recreation can be developed as a complement to safeguarding and enhancing the natural environment. National Trails are one means of facilitating public access and informal recreation.

Policy Q7

A multi-purpose countryside should be secured and where necessary investment and renewal in rural areas should be encouraged. The quality and character of the rural environment should be maintained and enhanced, while securing necessary change to meet the economic and social needs of local people and visitors. Special consideration should be given to the economic and social needs of the Rural Priority Areas.

a   Development plans should:

   i   encourage investment in rural towns and villages to help provide and maintain a range of local services, cultural facilities and employment opportunities for the local community;

   ii   encourage farm based diversification to allow the development of alternative sources of income and employment for those in rural areas. In particular, initiatives which would add value to the agricultural product of the farm, provide for tourism, leisure and cultural activities or other appropriate economic activities, should be promoted.

Local authorities should ensure that the scale of any diversification activity is appropriate to its setting and that proposals do not lead to an unacceptable impact on the local transport network or landscape character;

iii encourage good quality development which contributes to local distinctiveness and reflects national guidance in PPG7 *(The Countryside – Environmental Quality and Economic and Social Development)* on the location and scale of development in rural areas, including the reuse and adaptation of rural buildings; and

iv safeguard the setting and character of historic towns and villages. Further guidance is provided in chapter 6 of this guidance.

b In addition:

i Regional Development Agencies, the Countryside Agency, local authorities and other regional and local partners need to work together to develop programmes encouraging enterprise in the rural economy as well as integrated initiatives to sustain diverse rural communities; and

ii these partners should, where appropriate and eligible, take advantage of grant schemes which form part of the England Rural Development Programme. This Programme explains how the Government intends to use funding available as part of the European Union's Rural Development Regulation and sets out a list of objectives and priorities for rural development in the South East.

Sustaining Rural Communities

5.22 In view of the relative remoteness of rural areas and the smaller population catchments, it is essential for regional and local partners to continue also to develop innovative solutions to ensure the provision of community services and public transport in rural areas. Local people must have access to services such as healthcare, schools and shops, as well as convenient transport, a range of job opportunities and quality housing in order to help rural areas thrive. Further advice, specifically on affordable housing, is set out in chapter 8 of this guidance.

Policy Q8

A more equitable, and locally based, provision of services (including education and health, recreation, leisure, transport and cultural facilities) should also be achieved in rural areas.

a Development plans, and where relevant local transport plans, should:

i include policies and proposals for the provision for services within rural areas, particularly through support for the role of market towns as a focus for services and facilities. For example, encouraging mixed use developments which incorporate health care provision with other uses;

ii ensure that employment, services and facilities are sited in accessible rural locations;

iii clarify the inter-relationships between rural settlements and urban areas; and

iv contain policies and proposals which cater for both the needs of the rural population and the needs of tourists, whilst protecting the character of the countryside and promoting safe routes for walking and cycling.

b In addition, local authorities and relevant partners, should:

i develop innovative approaches to managing transport demand in rural areas. For example, the shared use of existing services such as post and school buses and mobile libraries or the use of telecommunications infrastructure to help address the problems of remoteness;

ii make use of the range of tools now available to help establish and meet the needs and aspirations of rural areas. Initiatives such as Rural Strategies, Planning for Real, Village Appraisals and Village Design Statements as well as local authority community strategies can help involve a wide section of the local community in working with local authorities, health, education and other service providers, the private sector, the Countryside Agency and other Government agencies to bring forward sensitive development planning in rural areas;

iii develop locally agreed strategies to assist in the delivery of sensitively designed affordable housing to meet local needs. Further advice on affordable housing is contained in chapter 8; and

iv take steps, as in urban areas, to ensure that crime prevention considerations are incorporated in the design of new development in rural areas (refer to policy Q2).

Chapter 6

Environmental Strategy and the Countryside

6.1 A high quality environment is essential to the future prosperity of the South East. The effective protection of the environment and prudent use of natural resources are fundamental aspects of the vision for this Region which is highly urbanised and subject to development pressures. This chapter encourages regional partners in planning positively for the care and management of the Region's environment. Climate change in the future may have unpredictable impacts, ranging from coastal inundation to habitat displacement to suit the new climate. It is, therefore, all the more important to continue to monitor environmental changes.

Areas of International and National Importance for Nature Conservation, Landscape and Cultural Value

6.2 Throughout the Region significant areas of land are statutorily designated in recognition of their intrinsic environmental, wildlife, landscape or cultural value. For example, the Region hosts a number of internationally important wildlife sites, designated under the terms of the Ramsar Convention and the European Habitats and Birds Directive. These areas are shown on Map 3. Development likely to affect such sites must be subject to stringent assessment in accordance with the Conservation (Natural Habitats and Conservation) Regulations 1994. With respect to the New Forest and the South Downs, the Government has asked the Countryside Agency to explore the designation of these areas as National Parks.

Policy E1

Priority should be given to protecting areas designated at international or national level either for their intrinsic nature conservation value, their landscape quality or their cultural importance.

a   Development plans should:

   i   accord with guidance in PPG9 *(Nature Conservation)* in protecting and enhancing areas which are designated for their:

   • intrinsic environmental value of international importance - RAMSAR Sites, Special Protection Areas (SPAs) Special Areas of Conservation (SACs);

   • intrinsic environmental value of national importance - National Nature Reserves (NNRs), Sites of Special Scientific Interest (SSSIs);

ii accord with guidance in PPG7 *(The Countryside – Environmental Quality and Economic and Social Development)* and PPG15 *(Planning and the Historic Environment)* and PPG16 *(Archaeology and Planning)* in protecting and enhancing existing and new areas designated for their:

- landscape value – Areas of Outstanding Natural Beauty (AONBs), New Forest Heritage Area (including the small area within Wiltshire), National Parks;

- cultural value – Scheduled Ancient Monuments (SAMs), World Heritage Sites; and

iii ensure that in their area or sector based policies and proposals, they reflect the priorities for protection of internationally and nationally designated areas.

b In addition, local authorities and other partners should make use of a range of management arrangements in place throughout the Region for different designated areas. These include various forms of local partnership arrangements involving bodies such as English Nature, the Countryside Agency, county wildlife trusts and local authorities. In particular, voluntary agreements are operated between the Ministry of Agriculture, Fisheries and Food and farmers in the designated Environmentally Sensitive Areas for an enhanced regime of countryside conservation.

Biodiversity

6.3 The Region possesses a wide range of habitats, including heathland, downland, meadows, ancient semi-natural woodland, rivers and wetlands. The Government is signatory to international agreements and is committed to safeguarding biological diversity. This involves diversity within species, between species and of ecosystems. The Government has endorsed the UK Biodiversity Action Plan (BAP) containing specific action plans for some 400 priority species and 45 key habitats. The species and habitat plans set out the national priorities and targets, but the process is also being taken forward locally through Local Biodiversity Action Plans (LBAPs). These are being prepared across the Region by Steering Groups involving English Nature, other Government agencies, wildlife trusts, local authorities and other partners. They are important in setting strategic and local targets which should inform development plans and other strategies.

6.4 Given the extent of agricultural activity in terms of land area in the South East, agricultural activity is a major influence on biodiversity. The England Rural Development Plan will encourage land management regimes that are sympathetic to wildlife. Regional targets are being developed for the area covered by the Government Office for the South East through the South East England Biodiversity Framework and will inform the Regional Sustainable Development Framework. The East of England Biodiversity Forum is currently working on a biodiversity audit of the East of England. The Greater London Authority Act 1999 also requires the Mayor to prepare a Biodiversity Action Plan and to have regard to this in preparing other strategies including the Spatial Development Strategy.

Policy E2

The Region's biodiversity should be maintained and enhanced with positive action to achieve the targets set in national and local biodiversity action plans through planning decisions and other measures.

a Development plans should give priority to specific species and habitats of international, national and sub-regional importance as identified in Biodiversity Action Plans (BAPs) and include policies and proposals to contribute to the achievement of targets set in BAPs by:

i   conserving and enhancing existing wildlife habitats in both urban and rural areas;

ii   encouraging the identification and management of existing and potential land for nature conservation as part of development proposals, particularly where a connected series of sites can be achieved; and

iii identifying locations and proposals for habitat management, restoration and creation schemes.

b   In addition:

i   the presence of a protected species is a material consideration in considering development proposals. Further guidance is provided in PPG9 *(Nature Conservation)*;

ii   local authorities should continue to co-operate with other agencies in the formulation of LBAPs and LEAPs (Local Environment Agency Plans);

iii local authorities and other public bodies can set an example for others by the way in which they manage their own landholdings; and

iv   agri-environment measures such as the Countryside Stewardship Scheme and Environmentally Sensitive Area designations, are important in safeguarding and enhancing biodiversity. The impact of these and future schemes should be monitored closely and measures adjusted accordingly.

Green Belts

6.5   The Region has extensive Green Belt coverage, with the Metropolitan Green Belt around London, Metropolitan Open Land within London and also Green Belts in South West Hampshire and around Oxford, as indicated on Map 3. Green Belts have long been an essential policy tool for containing urban sprawl. Detailed guidance is set out in PPG2 *(Green Belts)* and included in RPG3 *(Strategic Guidance for London)*. The Government believes that the designated Green Belts in the South East continue to be important in preventing urban sprawl, in preventing the coalescence of settlements and in protecting the countryside. Furthermore, they assist urban renaissance strategies. The Government does not believe that there is a regional case for reviewing the existing Green Belt boundaries, although it is recognised that where settlements are tightly constrained by the Green Belt, local circumstances may suggest the need for a review after urban capacity studies have been undertaken and the local authorities have considered all other alternative locations for development within their area.

Policy E3

There is no regional case for reviewing Green Belt boundaries in the light of this strategy.

a   In preparing development plans local authorities should:

i   frame policies in accordance with advice in PPG2 *(Green Belts)*. Where there are local exceptional circumstances which justify a review of Green Belt boundaries, such a review should follow the advice set out in PPG2. Such a review should also take account of sustainability criteria including: proximity to urban areas well served by public transport, environmental quality of the land and the contribution made by the Green Belt to the planning objectives for the area.

b   In addition:

i   local authorities should continue to work with other agencies, private partners and landowners to encourage appropriate uses of land; and

ii   the implementation of positive management schemes is also vital to improve the landscape, nature conservation and environmental value, as well as assisting agriculture and recreational activities within Green Belts, particularly where they adjoin built-up areas.

Wider Countryside Including Coastal and River Environment

6.6   In addition to nationally and internationally designated areas, the wider countryside of the South East is valuable in providing countryside around and between towns, undeveloped coast, extensive open space and river corridors. The River Thames, in particular, is a major leisure and recreation resource of international significance for wildlife and heritage, as well as being an important working river. It is the subject of more detailed guidance in RPG3b/9b *(Strategic Planning Guidance for the River Thames)*.

6.7   Many local authorities have introduced local designations such as Areas of Great Landscape Value or Strategic Gaps as a means of protecting areas of countryside for various purposes. PPG7 *(The Countryside - Environmental Quality and Economic and Social Development)* advises that in reviewing their development plans local authorities should rigorously consider the function and justification for existing designations and ensure that they are soundly based on a formal assessment of the qualities of the countryside or the contribution of such areas to urban form. The Countryside Character analysis and Natural Area Profiles devised by English Nature and the Countryside Agency in association with English Heritage, can provide a useful understanding of the qualities of different areas of the countryside and the basis for formulating sensitive design policies.

6.8   For other key elements of the Region's environment, there are a number of designations and management tools to focus effort and resources. In relation to coastal planning, these include the Heritage Coasts which are identified on Map 3, where a balance is needed between the requirements of conservation and access in the coastal zone. Further guidance is contained in PPG20 *(Coastal Planning)*. In relation to woodlands, Community Forests provide one means of promoting new woodland planting (see Map 3). Together with existing woodland, they will help to contribute to the delivery of the *England Forestry Strategy* and a significant increase in woodland cover, regulating air quality and providing a potential source of coppice timber for renewable energy resources.

6.9   The tranquillity, quality and variety of the Region's countryside, including villages, country estates and a range of cultural attractions, provide a major leisure asset for both inhabitants and visitors. If managed appropriately, both formal and informal leisure and recreation can be developed as a complement to safeguarding and enhancing the natural environment. For example, National Trails are one means of facilitating public access and informal recreation.

Policy E4

The landscape, wildlife, natural character and built heritage qualities of the coastal zone should be protected and enhanced, especially those areas designated as Heritage Coast.

a   Development plans should:

i   reflect advice contained in PPG20 *(Coastal Planning)* in identifying different types of coast (Heritage Coast, designated, undeveloped, developed and despoiled) and providing appropriate policies for the safeguarding, development, enhancement and regeneration of coastal zones;

ii   adopt an integrated approach to the future management of coastal areas, including the identification of major areas of coastal land at risk from substantial erosion or other physical constraints such as land instability, measures to alleviate such problems e.g.

protection works and defence works, on-shore/off-shore development pressures, sources of coastal pollution and opportunities for more environmentally sensitive uses; and

    iii   include policies for the enhancement of degraded coastal areas, especially in the PAERs.

b   In addition:

    i   Estuary Management Plans, Coastal Zone Management Plans and Shoreline Management Plans can be used to promote sustainable development in coastal areas. They need to take account of the need to balance competing uses including nature conservation, port development, mineral extraction, marinas, power stations and other uses. In particular, designated coastal areas as shown on Map 3 need to be managed positively;

    ii   management proposals will also need to reflect strategies agreed between relevant bodies, including the Environment Agency for flood defence and district councils involved in coastal protection. Further guidance on coastal flooding is included in chapter 10; and

    iii   regional partners need to find ways of monitoring long term changes to the shape of the coastline.

Policy E5

Woodland habitats in the Region should be increased whilst protecting the biodiversity and character of existing woodland resources and other areas of established or potential nature conservation value.

a   Development plans should:

    i   promote the retention, protection and extension of woodland and forest habitats, particularly ancient and semi-natural woodlands and also Community Forests; and

    ii   identify the scope for woodland creation, for example, in association with the restoration of degraded landscapes, particularly in the Thames Gateway and PAERs.

b   In addition:

    i   forest and woodland strategies drawn up in partnership between the Forestry Commission, local authorities and others, can help to improve woodland management. For example, by promoting planting of broadleaved species, by enabling the use of woodlands as a community resource and by developing the potential supply of timber for renewable energy or other productive uses; and

    ii   use should be made of advice available from the National Urban Forestry Unit on how to integrate woodland planting in regeneration strategies, for example, to enhance the prospects of redeveloping vacant or derelict land.

Policy E6

Opportunities should be provided for leisure and recreation in, and access to, the countryside in ways which retain and enhance its character.

a   Development plans should:

    i   maximise the use of highly managed areas such as regional parks, country parks, national trails, cultural attractions and sports facilities;

ii   ensure that in more sensitive locations new facilities are only provided for less intensive leisure and recreation activities, and only where appropriate and sustainable locations exist;

iii   maximise the positive benefits of sport, leisure, recreation and cultural development for the rural environment, local communities, local economy and visitors; and

iv   reflect guidance contained in PPG7 *(The Countryside – Environmental Quality and Economic and Social Development)*, PPG17 *(Sport and Recreation)*, PPG20 *(Coastal Planning)* and PPG21 *(Tourism)*.

b   In addition:

i   access to existing and new leisure, recreation and cultural facilities and the Rights of Way network will require continued improvement so that visitors and all members of the local community, including the physically impaired, can participate in rural sports, informal recreation and cultural activities; and

ii   recreational activities need to be directed to sustainable locations and in ways which respect the agricultural, biodiversity, landscape and heritage value of the countryside.

Air and water quality

6.10   Ultimately, the quality of the Region's environment is underpinned by the key elements of air, water, land, soil and the extent to which the design of development is sensitive to the natural environment. Policy advice on water quality is provided in chapter 10 of this guidance.

6.11   Air quality in the Region has improved over recent decades with respect to domestic sources. However, vehicle emissions, energy generation and industrial processes continue to contribute to air pollution. The *Air Quality Strategy for England, Scotland, Wales and Northern Ireland* sets out measures for reducing the emissions of eight main pollutants and promotes the integration of land use planning and pollution control. Local authorities throughout the Region are working with the Environment Agency and other partners across local administrative boundaries, in monitoring air quality and devising management strategies. Local authorities have the opportunity to improve air quality both directly and as a result of other functions such as land use planning. The Greater London Authority Act 1999 requires the Mayor to prepare a London Air Quality strategy. London local authorities must have regard to this strategy when carrying out their duties under the local air quality management system.

Policy E7

Local authorities should work with the Environment Agency and others to play a positive part in pollution control and encourage measures to improve air quality.

a   Development plans should:

i   include policies on the location of potentially polluting developments and the location of sensitive developments in the vicinity of existing polluting developments in line with guidance in PPG23 *(Planning and Pollution Control)*;

ii   take account of the findings of air quality reviews and assessments; and

iii   take into account any Air Quality Management Areas (AQMAs) designated under Part IV of the Environment Act 1995 and any AQMA action plans.

b   In addition, local authorities should:

i   ensure at the planning application stage, that air quality is taken into account where appropriate along with other material considerations;

ii   seek to reduce environmental impacts of transport activities by supporting the increased provision of cleaner transport fuels such as liquefied petroleum gas (LPG) and compressed natural gas (CNG), for example, by enabling the development of refuelling infrastructure; and

iii   work in partnership taking steps (indicated in Box 4) to achieve an integrated approach to air quality management.

Box 4 - Steps local authorities can take to improve local air quality:

- the prompt identification of Air Quality Management Areas and the drawing up of action plans to improve air quality in that locality;

- ensuring that air quality considerations are factored into decisions on transport, energy and land-use planning;

- working towards reductions in emissions from point sources of air pollution;

- working towards reductions in vehicle emissions through reducing travel demand and encouraging less-polluting vehicles;

- working with other local authorities, the highways authorities, representatives of the local community and the Environment Agency;

- building on business initiatives such as Travel Plans and establishing voluntary agreements;

- positive action to regulate and improve air quality through tree and woodland planting;

- informing and involving the public; and

- detailed and comprehensive monitoring of all pollutants of concern.

Source: In part from Draft RPG9 (SERPLAN, A Sustainable Development Strategy for the South East, 1998).

Soil and land quality

6.12   Soil has received little attention in the past despite its important role, including in the production of food, raw materials and energy and in providing a filtering and buffering action to protect water and the food chain from potential pollutants. In addition, different soils are part of ecosystems which help maintain gene pools and wildlife populations and so provide a basis for biodiversity. They also contain archaeological evidence of our history. The Government is preparing a soil strategy for England which will set out objectives and measures for soil protection. It will be important for local authorities to take account of this advice in preparing development plans. The protection of soils in the South East is important both in terms of supporting biodiversity and food production.

6.13   Land quality is considered in various ways including its value for agricultural production. The Agricultural Land Classification system is used to grade agricultural land and this forms the basis for classifying 'best and most versatile agricultural land'. Further guidance is provided in PPG7 *(The Countryside – Environmental Quality and Economic and Social Development)*.

6.14   In terms of the suitability of land for supporting built structures, advice is provided in PPG14 *(Development on Unstable Land)*. The use of geographic information systems and earth sciences is generating a growing volume of information about land quality, such as guidance on sources of earth science information for planning and development (R. Ellison & A Smith, 1998). Within the South East, for example, there are areas of potentially unstable land which need to be taken into account when planning land use and development. These may be associated with:

- landslides and falls of rock, particularly at eroding coastal slopes and cliffs or associated with certain clays of the lower Thames Valley, the Hampshire area and of the Weald; and

- small abandoned shallow mines, particularly in the Weald, North and South Downs and the Chilterns; and natural underground cavities formed by dissolving rock (mainly the chalk areas of the Chilterns and North and South Downs); solution cavities (in the Hythe Beds in Kent and Jurassic rocks in Oxfordshire); slippage of rock (in parts of Kent, Sussex and Oxfordshire); and marine erosion (the chalk coasts of Kent and Sussex).

6.15 Many areas of unstable land, such as those associated with cliffs, also have a high nature conservation value so that they need to be safeguarded in accordance with guidance on biodiversity and other policies in this guidance.

Policy E8

Valuable characteristics of soil and land should be protected.

a   Development plans should:

   i   set out policies on the level of protection to be afforded to the best and most versatile agricultural land;

   ii   ensure that soils are protected so that they can perform a range of important functions, such as the support of diverse habitats and thus contribute to biodiversity; and

   iii include policies for preventing building upon unstable land unless adequate measures are put in place in accordance with guidance in PPG14 *(Development on Unstable Land)*.

b   In addition:

   i   agri-environment measures such as Environmentally Sensitive Areas and the Countryside Stewardship scheme can help secure diverse landscapes and biodiversity on agricultural land;

   ii   organic farming and other less intensive agricultural practices will also have an impact on soil quality; and

   iii where soil and land have been degraded, local partners, with the assistance of Government agencies, should maximise the opportunities for restoration and habitat creation schemes.

Chapter 7

The Regional Economy

7.1 The Government has a range of policies to help UK business compete more effectively in global markets. The planning system can support these policies. It can guide development to locations that are sustainable in economic, social and environmental terms. This chapter sets out ways in which the development principles in chapter 3 and the spatial framework in chapter 4 can support the prosperity and international competitiveness of the South East and its contribution to the national economy.

Economic Success and Human Resources

7.2 The South East with London at its centre and good access to international markets, plays an important role in the national economy. It is a gateway to continental Europe. The Region has a network of world class universities and research institutions. Many of the world's leading companies have invested in the South East. It is strong in rapidly growing sectors such as business services, information and communications technology and biotechnology, and is well represented in more traditional service and manufacturing sectors. It has thriving arts and tourism sectors and a wide range of rural business activity. The South East is well placed, and has the human and commercial resource to grow and prosper. However, the Region is under-performing in European terms and parts of the Region are barely average in national terms. There are also housing and transport issues in parts of the Region that could, if they are not addressed, hold back its growth. These are addressed in subsequent chapters.

7.3 RPG3 *(Strategic Guidance for London Planning Authorities)* provides guidance in the development of London's economy. In London, the London Development Agency (LDA) is responsible for formulating and delivering the mayor's economic development and regeneration strategy. The Regional Development Agencies, SEEDA and EEDA, have published Regional Economic Strategies for the rest of the South East which aim to improve the economic performance of the South East and East of England regions. One of their key objectives is to promote high value added growth centred on the new knowledge-based industries. New development needs to maximise the opportunities for urban renaissance, travel by non-car modes, the re-use of previously developed land and opportunities for all sections of the workforce.

Policy RE1

The regional economy should be supported and further developed to ensure that it contributes fully to national growth and follows the principles of sustainable development.

a   Development plans should:

    i   take account of the Regional Economic Strategies and develop complementary sustainable land use policies and proposals including the identification of locations for growing businesses and inward investors;

    ii   have regard to guidance on sustainable development contained in PPG1 *(General Policy and Principles)*; and

    iii   within London, implement the guidance set out in RPG3 and consider forthcoming strategies to be prepared by the London Development Agency.

b   In addition:

    i   the Regional Development Agencies are working together with local authorities, economic partnerships and business organisations to address needs of local business, potential growth sectors and potential inward investors through the development and implementation of their Regional Economic Strategies;

    ii   businesses and other employers will be able to devise sustainable location strategies which take account of these economic strategies and also social and environmental factors; and

    iii   local authorities should continue to work with relevant partners in preparing complementary local transport, housing and skills strategies to ensure that development is sustainable.

Policy RE2

Human resource development should be recognised as a central component in harnessing and promoting future economic success in the Region and access to job opportunities should be improved for those currently disadvantaged in the labour market.

a   Development plans should include policies which ensure that sufficient and accessible premises are available for training and education purposes to suit the requirements identified through the relevant strategies, including those to be drawn up by Learning and Skills Councils and the Regional Economic Strategies.

b   In addition:

    i   the Employment Service, Learning and Skills Councils, local learning partnerships and local employers play important roles in enhancing skills and opportunities in the Region;

    ii   further and higher educational establishments are also vital to the success of training and education strategies;

    iii   local authorities should consider how they can support similar measures to those already employed by some of the best universities and colleges in establishing effective links with knowledge based industries; and

    iv   in order to assist access to job opportunities, the scope for the provision of training and childcare facilities in association with development should be explored through the use of Section 106 agreements between local authorities and developers, following advice set out in Circular 1/97 *(Planning Obligations).*

Policy RE3

A long-term and holistic approach should be taken to economic development activities.

a   Development plans should:

    i   take full account of local economic development strategies, which will need to reflect local capacity in terms of labour, land availability and transport infrastructure, build upon local strengths, including skills, local research strengths, and strong business clusters, and should reflect changing work and living patterns; and

ii   include policies to help sustain economic activity and encourage enterprise in rural areas.

b   In addition:

i   Regional Development Agencies, business support organisations, economic partnerships and local authorities all have a role to play in developing comprehensive and holistic economic development strategies;

ii   local authorities, Regional Development Agencies and other regional partners should consider how they can facilitate partnerships with residents and business interests to encourage community based economic development, ensuring that training and skill requirements are effectively identified and focussed on the needs of the local economy; and

iii   business support organisations can make a significant contribution in helping businesses to become actively involved in the local planning process.

Policy RE4

Business should be encouraged in adopting the principles of sustainable development.

a   Development plans should:

i   include policies which reduce business related travel, for example, ensuring that businesses are located in areas well served or capable of being well served by sustainable modes of transport and requiring travel plans for all substantial new travel generating developments; and

ii   encourage forms of development which maximise environmental and social benefits, for example, mixed use development which links housing and employment, and which integrate energy efficient design.

b   In addition, business support organisations and such networks as Local Agenda 21, can do much to assist local companies in understanding the nature and long-term benefits of environmentally sound business practices. For example, by encouraging businesses in the prudent use of natural resources, in contributing to increased biodiversity and in minimising, reusing and recycling of waste materials.

Making the best use of land resources

7.4   As a densely populated and developed Region, the South East has an extensive range of premises and sites. Factors such as changes in the fortunes of different sectors and the evolution of information technology will affect the amount of space and location of premises demanded by businesses. This can lead to some sites being abandoned and left derelict, while elsewhere attractive landscapes may be under pressure for development. It is important to enable flexibility in the range of premises available while at the same time ensuring that better use is made of existing developed land. Further guidance on the location of industrial and commercial development is contained in PPG1 *(General Policy and Principles)*, PPG4 *(Industrial and Commercial Development and Small Firms)*, PPG6 *(Town Centres and Retail Development)*, PPG11 *(Regional Planning)*, PPG12 *(Development Plans)* and Draft PPG13 *(Transport)*.

Policy RE5

Better use should be made of existing employment land resources. Sites for industry and commerce should be developed particularly in urban areas and in places which are accessible by environmentally friendly modes of transport. Precedence should be given to the re-use of developed land over the release of new land and wherever possible the intensification of use on existing sites should be encouraged.

a   Development plans should:

   i   allocate employment land within an overall strategy for urban renaissance and rural development, providing a range of premises and sites to meet the varied needs of business;

   ii   include policies and proposals which result from a review of existing and potential sites considering various factors including:

   • current use and scope for intensification;

   • scope for optimising the use of previously developed land;

   • scope for mixing employment uses with other land uses such as housing and education;

   • availability of land within built up urban areas suitable for development and redevelopment;

   • potential for increasing access by sustainable transport modes;

   • marketability; and

   • the resources required to bring sites forward for development.

b   In addition:

   i   Regional Development Agencies, economic partnerships, businesses and others need to have regard to this guidance in developing strategies for growing indigenous businesses and targeting suitable inward investment; and

   ii   it is important for business interests to appraise local authorities of changing spatial requirements of business and to seek innovative solutions jointly.

Economic Distribution in the Region

7.5   Overall the South East has a buoyant and successful economy. However, parts of the Region do not show the same sustained economic progress as others and stand in need of further development. This section distinguishes the approaches to economic development which are relevant to the different parts of the Region identified in chapters 4 and 12 of this guidance.

Policy RE6

Priority should be given to securing economic development in the Thames Gateway in accordance with the guidance and principles set out in RPG9a or in any review of RPG9a. To ensure balanced and sustainable development, there is a need for inward investment to be supported by adequate transport and community infrastructure and housing provision.

a   Development plans should:

   i   continue to pursue the implementation of proposals identified in RPG9a with emphasis on ensuring good design combined with efficient use of land, integration of transport and land use, and mixed use development wherever possible;

ii   identify additional opportunities for employment uses, with the potential for integration with good transport access, housing and services while enhancing the natural environment; and

iii   maximise opportunities for improving access within the Thames Gateway, particularly by non-car modes, with close co-operation between adjoining authorities.

b   In addition:

i   the new Strategic Partnership will be able to consider ways of enhancing the co-ordination and delivery of programmes and strategies in the Thames Gateway;

ii   the Regional Development Agencies, together with local authorities, private interests and other key partners, will be able to reflect the regional and national priority of the Thames Gateway in their implementation and investment strategies, including the targeting of inward investment;

iii   comprehensive marketing and redevelopment strategies involving an ongoing dialogue with potential developers are important elements for the success of the Thames Gateway; and

iv   close co-operation between the various organisations will be helpful in developing training strategies for the local workforce and strategies for increasing the capacity of local communities to achieve the regeneration of their areas.

Policy RE7

In order to address strategic spatial inequalities around the Region, local and regional partners should also give particular attention to actively supporting economic regeneration and renewal, including inward investment in Priority Areas for Economic Regeneration (PAERs).

a   PAERs are listed in chapter 4 and referred to in more detail in chapter 12 of this guidance. Within PAERs, development plans should:

i   contain integrated policies for transport, housing, employment and educational facilities, which will tackle the identified economic weaknesses of the PAERs, reflect the regional priority for investment in these areas and are consistent with local economic development and regeneration strategies;

ii   review the amount and type of employment land available in the light of local employment needs and the needs of inward investors;

iii   identify strategic sites for commercial development with the potential for good transport access, including links with airports;

iv   review existing employment sites and consider whether any upgrading or improvement is required to meet the needs of the type of business that is needed in the area; and

v   ensure full advantage is taken of economic strengths and opportunities in the area including transport links, local knowledge and skills and existing and potential business clusters.

b   In addition:

i   Regional Development Agencies, local authorities, Learning and Skills Councils and other regional partners all have an interest in working together on regeneration strategies for individual PAERs. These will help assist the local workforce to gain the skills needed by existing and potential employers; and

ii   local strategic partnerships can increase the community capacity to achieve regeneration.

7.6 The Western Policy Area is economically buoyant and it is important that growth continues in a way which minimises the additional pressure on land and labour resources. High value added activities are likely to be particularly important. The growing economy has led to the development of 'hotspots' or localised areas of problems. Indicators which local authorities could use to define such areas include: significant traffic congestion, high employment growth and significant labour shortages, the extent to which land is under pressure as balanced against environmental criteria which may be manifested in a rapid growth in prices of residential or commercial properties. This part of the Region requires effective management of local areas with clear plan-led strategies underpinned by a sound understanding of an area's economic strengths and weaknesses and effective use of local resources to build upon those strengths. The local authorities with the support of the Regional Development Agencies, face the challenge of enabling continued economic prosperity in this area while discouraging new development of a type which would be unsustainable.

Policy RE8

In the Western Policy Area, positive strategies should be developed for areas where congestion or labour or land shortages are constraining economic growth. 'Hotspots' should be identified and specific policies developed to tackle local problems.

a   Development plans should:

   i   ensure that the best use is made of employment land to maximise the performance of the economy as a whole, facilitating changes of use of land where appropriate and ensuring that land allocations and development policies are consistent with local economic development strategies;

   ii   identify hotspots and formulate specific policies and proposals to tackle the problems in these localised areas. This might include:

- re-allocating land where necessary to secure a better balance between housing and employment;

- tighter traffic management and parking policies including a co-ordinated approach to travel plans;

- additional investment in public transport provision and facilities for walking and cycling; and

- greater emphasis on affordable housing based on local need assessments.

b   In addition, local authorities should:

   i   work with partners to tackle congestion through local transport and housing strategies which secure private contributions to add value to public investment. This would include focusing priorities for investment in Local Transport Plans and encouraging public-private partnership; and

   ii   consider undertaking an audit of outstanding commitments and current stock of employment land in accordance with criteria set out in policy RE5 of this guidance with particular emphasis on accessibility by non-road transport alternatives.

Business Clusters

7.7 The future economic success for the South East will depend on taking advantage of and enhancing the Region's existing strengths, including the Region's enterprise and innovation culture. The background to achieving this is the rapidly developing global market, where competitive advantage derives from knowledge as well as cost. To help them succeed in this demanding environment, businesses are increasingly working together to their mutual advantage and many have formed clusters.

7.8 Typically a cluster would involve a geographic concentration of interconnected companies, specialised suppliers, service providers, firms in related industries and associated research and other institutions. Such clusters may extend across several local authority boundaries. Government has commissioned a national study on the mapping of clusters. This will help inform Regional Development Agencies in the implementation of their Regional Economic Strategies. Within the South East there are clusters in a range of sectors including the pharmaceutical industries, business services, biotechnology, motorsports, telecommunications and the creative industries. The planning system can play a part in facilitating the development of clusters, for example, with regard to premises and access. Issues such the flexibility of property leases and effective use of infrastructure are also aspects which could assist the development of clusters. Further guidance is provided in PPG12 *(Development plans)*.

Policy RE9

High value-added activities should be actively encouraged, including the grouped location of such activities in business clusters where this is economically beneficial and environmentally acceptable.

a   Development plans should include policies which serve to encourage existing and emerging clusters and which promote the diffusion of innovation throughout the Region, particularly in the Thames Gateway and PAERs. This might include, identifying science and technology parks that are well served by sustainable modes of transport and close to universities or research facilities, identifying networks of sites linked by telecommunications, proposing sites for incubator units, proposing sites for small and growing businesses and identifying potential locations for corporate headquarters.

b   With the benefit of such policies in development plans, Regional Development Agencies, business support organisations, higher and further education establishments and others will be able to maximise the potential of key activities and clusters for the local and regional economies. A culture of innovation and effective use of new technology will be facilitated in which there can be continued partnership working to encourage diversification and modernisation of existing business, for example, through better links with research and development facilities.

c   In monitoring and reviewing this guidance the Regional Planning Bodies, Mayor of London and the Regional Development Agencies should consider existing and potential clusters of regional significance that may require additional support infrastructure.

Economic Diversity

7.9 It is important to encourage all aspects of the economy and ensure that the economy remains broadly based. Sustainable local economies are ones with strong local supply chains which support emerging and established companies. A balanced economy requires a range of types of employment space in terms of size, location and cost. Some of this space will need to accommodate uses which may be labour intensive but low value in terms of wealth generation.

7.10　In addition to the growth sectors of the economy, it is also important to retain sectors such as manufacturing and warehousing, which are not expected to provide additional employment on a large scale in the future. New sources of demand for industrial land, especially in urban areas, may arise from the development of new products such as those derived from recycled materials or appliances which enable more efficient use of water and energy. Throughout the Region a substantial proportion of future employment growth in the South East is expected to take place through growth in the number of small and medium enterprises (SMEs).

7.11　Tourism and the arts, culture and media are significant elements of the Region's economy and are predicted to become major growth sectors. The South East has an excellent foundation for the development of employment in these sectors. Key features include London as a centre for national administration, entertainment, tourism and culture; coastal and marine-based attractions; environmental and rural attractions; national heritage sites and museums; historic towns and cities and major sporting and musical events. Opportunities are further enhanced by the potential for extensive transport infrastructure and a large population within and close to the Region.

Policy RE10

Economic diversity should be encouraged, facilitating small and medium enterprises, and supporting the growth of a variety of economic sectors including manufacturing.

a　In preparing development plans, local authorities should:

　　i　assess the requirements of the various sectors of the local economy and ensure that provision is made for a balanced economy in both urban and rural areas;

　　ii　provide for a range of sites for small and medium sized businesses including, for example, incubator units and innovation centres; and

　　iii　in areas with an over-dependence on one sector such as the service sector, take specific action to preserve industrial sites where a need for such sites has been identified.

Policy RE11

Tourism, arts and culture should be encouraged.

b　Development plans should:

　　i　include policies to promote tourism, arts and cultural activities. In particular, they should ensure that existing and new facilities are readily accessible by sustainable modes of transport and that tourism, arts and culture contribute to the regeneration of the Thames Gateway and PAERs; and

　　ii　have regard to Government guidance in PPG17 *(Sport and Recreation)*, PPG21 *(Tourism)* and RPG3 *(Strategic Guidance for London Planning Authorities)*.

b　Regional Cultural Consortia are developing their cultural strategies which will inform and be informed by local cultural strategies. They will identify priorities for all cultural and creative interests including tourism. In addition tourist boards will further develop their tourism strategies. These can benefit through close working with local authorities and Regional Development Agencies in encouraging appropriate tourist facilities based on local attractions and activities whilst protecting the local environment and infrastructure from unacceptable pressures.

c　In line with advice in PPG11 *(Regional Planning)*, the Regional Planning Bodies and the Mayor of London should, as part of the review of this guidance, have regard to regional cultural strategies and develop more regionally specific guidance on tourism, including links with sport and recreation facilities.

Chapter 8

Housing

8.1 The Government's intention is that everyone should have the opportunity of a decent home. As set out in chapters 1 to 4 the general thrust of this guidance is towards a concentrated rather than dispersed pattern of development, with the emphasis on new dwelling provision being accommodated in urban areas in ways which enhance the quality of urban living. This involves making better use of the existing housing stock, along with re-use of vacant and under-used buildings and sites. Responding to need also requires better information on the requirements of different households and how these might be met by different types of housing. A substantial element of the additional housing required in the South East needs to be affordable, particularly for the most vulnerable households in the Region.

Housing Provision and Distribution

8.2 It is the function of RPG to set out a clear spatial strategy, including the distribution of housing requirements across the Region, taking into account all the relevant factors. This guidance sets out the housing requirements based on a 'Plan, Monitor and Manage' approach as outlined in PPG3 *(Housing)*. In determining the overall level of housing provision in the South East, and its distribution, account has been taken of the present and likely future pattern of housing need, including such factors as:

- the role of housing in supporting the Region's economy, especially in maintaining labour supply;

- projections of households in the Region, and how these translate to the need for dwellings;

- any indicators of outstanding need and housing shortfall;

- the interrelationship between London and ROSE;

- patterns of past completions and the condition of stock; and

- vacant dwellings and second homes.

Account has also been taken of the need to protect and enhance the Region's environment, the objectives for sustainable development and key development principles set out in chapter 3 and the core strategy in chapter 4 of this guidance.

8.3 Recent housing completions in ROSE have averaged about 39,000 dwellings a year. Consideration of the above factors suggests that the rate of completions should be increased in future years. However, until assessments have been completed of the capacity of urban areas and the scope for the potential growth areas to accommodate additional development, it is premature to specify precisely the increased level of provision and how it might be distributed, although it would be expected to result in around 43,000 dwellings a year. Future development needs to be achieved without perpetuating the trend to more dispersed and land-extensive patterns of development, especially as the population is likely to consist of a higher proportion of one- and two-person households. It should be possible through a plan-led process, to provide more dwellings than have been provided in recent years with proportionately less impact on land and other resources. For example, through development plan policies which exercise more control over the layout and type of housing and ensure a more efficient use of land.

8.4 In London, RPG3 already provides policies for an increase in housing provision within the overall requirement of the existing RPG9. Recent studies have shown the scope for significant increases in the capacity to a level where the capital could provide homes for about 23,000 additional households annually. This level of provision includes an allowance for additional non self contained accommodation and a reduction in the vacancy rate, in addition to the provision of new dwellings which will make up the bulk of the provision. In broad terms this rate of provision should accommodate London's anticipated household growth, but this assumption will be tested as part of the monitoring and review of this guidance. Policies to secure this level of provision and to guide its distribution, need to be included by the Mayor of London in the Spatial Development Strategy which will replace RPG3. Further guidance on this is set out in Circular 1/2000 (*Strategic Planning in London*).

Policy H1

In London, provision should be made to accommodate on average an additional 23,000 households yearly. In the Rest of the South East (ROSE) provision should be made for an annual average rate of 39,000 net additional dwellings. These levels of provision apply to the period between 2001 and 2006 and are subject to review before 2006 in the light of monitoring and the findings of the urban capacity studies and studies of potential growth areas.

Policy H2

The Mayor of London's Spatial Development Strategy, which will replace RPG3, should include guidance on how the additional 23,000 households being accommodated annually, will be distributed within London. In ROSE, development plans should make provision for net additional dwellings so as to achieve the following annual average level of provision:

County	Annual Average Rate
Bedfordshire	2,430
Berkshire	2,620
Buckinghamshire	3,210
East Sussex	2,290
Essex	5,240
Hampshire	6,030
Hertfordshire	3,280
Isle of Wight	520
Kent	5,700
Oxfordshire	2,430
Surrey	2,360
West Sussex	2,890

a   These rates of provision should apply to the period up to 2006. Where development plans are reviewed and the new plan extends beyond 2006, they should continue to provide for additional dwellings at the same annual average rate until such time as any different rate is adopted following review of this guidance.

b   Structure and unitary development plans should adopt the rates of provision set out in this guidance and consider distribution and the means of implementation. They should distribute the requirements within their plan area in accordance with this guidance and the principles of sustainable development. They should also follow the approach to planning for housing set out in PPG3 *(Housing)*.

c   Development plans should be updated as soon as possible in line with the guidance given in PPG12 *(Development Plans)* to ensure the speedy implementation of this distribution. In the meantime, proposals for development should have regard to this guidance.

Monitoring and Managing Housing Provision

8.5   The proposed dwelling requirements for London and ROSE follow the policy set out in PPG11 *(Regional Planning)* and PPG3 *(Housing)* that the planned level of housing provision should be based on the objectives of the strategy and linked to measurable indicators of change. The Government has not adjusted the housing provision to take account of the potential for further development in the Thames Gateway and the other areas of potential growth identified in this strategy over and above that already planned.

8.6   It is an essential feature of the plan, monitor and manage approach that housing provision and the ways of meeting it should be kept under continuous review at regional level. Appropriate indicators will need to be monitored by the Regional Planning Bodies and the Mayor of London and reported in annual monitoring reports. Monitoring needs to form the basis on which they periodically review and roll forward the housing strategy as part of the revised RPG and the Spatial Development Strategy for London. This should occur at a minimum every five years, and sooner if there are clear signs of either under- or over-provision of housing land.

Policy H3

The adequacy of this level of housing provision and distribution should be reviewed by regular monitoring of key indicators, in accordance with the guidance set out in PPG3 (*Housing*) and PPG11 (*Regional Planning*). The outcome of monitoring of these indicators should be reported in the Regional Planning Bodies' and Mayor of London's annual monitoring report and form the basis for decision on the timing of reviews of this guidance.

a   The Regional Planning Bodies and the Mayor of London, developers, house-builders, representatives of environmental organisations, and the Government Offices, should continue to discuss all the factors that contribute to the planning of housing requirements, with a view to the preparation of revised Draft Regional Planning Guidance or within London, a review of the Spatial Development Strategy, on the topic of housing as necessary and in any case within five years. The assessment of the required scale and distribution of housing should be kept under review so that any under- or over-provision can be corrected quickly. Monitoring of demographic and economic trends, housing needs, the use of the housing stock, the impact of development on environmental resources, or other factors, could singly or in combination, prompt a revision of this aspect of Regional Planning Guidance or within London, the Spatial Development Strategy.

b   In addition to monitoring and reviewing the housing requirement and the distribution set out above, the Regional Planning Bodies and the Mayor of London should initiate studies into the scope for and capacity of the Potential Growth Areas identified in chapter 4 for longer term planned growth. A higher rate of provision than 39,000 dwellings per annum is likely to be necessary to meet the long term needs in ROSE. Until the capacity of urban areas to accommodate additional development has been assessed throughout the Region and the scope for any additional development in the potential growth areas has been examined, it is premature to specify precisely what a different level of provision might be and how it would be distributed in a sustainable way, though it would be expected to result in around 43,000 dwellings a year.

Affordable Housing and Mixed Communities

8.7   It is evident from the results of local housing need assessment and also from feedback from employees that there is strong demand for affordable housing in the South East. Some employment and service sectors, for example the National Health Service, have difficulty recruiting and retaining key workers owing to the high cost of housing in the South East. A lack of affordable housing can also stimulate unsustainable long distance travel to work patterns if people cannot live near their work or in locations accessible to suitable public transport interchanges.

8.8   Future housing provision will also need to take account of patterns of household formation. Current household projections indicate that there is likely in future to be a higher proportion of one and two person households than at present. These households are likely to have different needs from larger households, in terms of the size, type and location of home required. Household projections, furthermore, indicate an increase in the proportion of households with older people. Inevitably there will also continue to be a need to be flexible in catering for various needs, such as the needs of people with disabilities.

8.9   The provision of affordable housing in the South East is an important component in the development of mixed and balanced communities, to help meet the housing needs of the whole population. Sufficient levels of affordable housing in the Region can allow all sectors of the community to have access to a decent home. It is vital to ensure the continued prosperity of the Region, by providing local firms and the private sector access to a wide cross section of the labour market.

8.10   In accordance with the strategy of urban renaissance it is clear that the majority of provision will need to be made within the existing urban fabric where opportunities are more likely to arise on smaller sites. The shortage of affordable housing in the rural areas also needs to be addressed.

8.11   The Government has consulted on its Housing Green Paper, published in April 2000. This set out a comprehensive strategy for ensuring that everyone has the opportunity of a decent home. Plans for taking forward the Green Paper proposals in the light of the consultation will be announced soon.

8.12   Public investment through local authorities and the Housing Corporation plays an important part in the delivery of new affordable housing, complementing planning powers for affordable housing. The Government's spending plans for housing over the next three years put in place the resources to deliver the strategy set out in the Green Paper. This includes the commitment to bring all social housing up to a decent standard within a decade. For new affordable housing, the plans include nearly doubling the Housing Corporation's programme so that, by 2003-04, annual capital investment in new social housing will be £1.2 billion. London and the South East will receive a substantial proportion of the Housing Corporation's programme, which is allocated according to housing need and regional priorities.

8.13 Local authorities also provide investment in new affordable housing (through Local Authority Social Housing Grant). Total capital allocations for local authority housing are being increased from £1.4 billion last year to £2.5 billion by 2003-04. In addition, the Government is making £250 million available over the next three years through its Starter Home Initiative. This will help key workers in high demand, high price areas like London and the South East to buy their own homes, where they might otherwise have been priced out of the communities they serve.

8.14 The planning system is also important in enabling the provision of affordable housing. Policies in development plans can assist delivery through securing an element of affordable housing as part of new development in accordance with advice in PPG3 *(Housing)* and Circular 6/98 *(Planning and Affordable Housing)*. Such policies also need to be supported by robust assessments of housing need across all tenures. The Government proposes to publish good practice guidance for local authorities and others on the delivery of affordable housing through planning policy. The Department of Environment, Transport and the Regions has already commissioned wide ranging research on the use of current planning policy to provide for affordable housing.

8.15 In this guidance, the term 'affordable housing' explicitly covers subsidised housing for rent and low-cost market housing in accordance with guidance set out in PPG3 *(Housing)* and Circular 6/98 *(Planning and Affordable Housing)*. The provision of both should be addressed through development plan policies. This definition is tenure neutral, and should be used in plans to encourage more mixed and balanced communities, and the provision of such housing by a variety of providers. Affordable housing requirements, in terms of tenure, size, type and location can then be addressed by means of local housing strategies backed up by a full assessment of need.

Policy H4

A range of dwelling types and sizes should be provided, including alternative forms of tenure, in order to meet the needs of all sectors of the community and to plan for balanced communities. Affordable housing should be provided to meet locally assessed need.

a Development plans should:

   i make provision for a range of dwelling types and sizes to meet the assessed needs of all sectors of the community, including elderly and disabled households;

   ii set out clearly the mix of dwelling types and sizes that would reasonably be expected in different locations of the authority's area against which development proposals can be assessed;

   iii include policies for securing affordable housing based on local housing strategies which in turn should be based on robust and regular local assessments of need;

   iv explain how the powers in Circular 6/98 *(Planning and Affordable Housing)* will be used to contribute towards meeting the local need for affordable housing, including setting indicative targets for the proportion of affordable housing on specific sites;

   v in rural areas, set appropriate thresholds for settlements with a population of 3,000 or less. Special rural measures such as the use of agricultural occupancy conditions or the 'exceptions' policy will continue to be appropriate in some circumstances; and

   vi ensure that affordable housing is provided where it is needed, in both urban and rural areas, and where appropriate located in mixed use developments, avoiding the creation of large housing areas of similar characteristics. In particular, affordable housing should be located where good public transport services provide links with employment opportunities, cultural facilities and other services such as leisure, education and healthcare.

b   Local authorities should also:

i   make use of supplementary planning guidance or site specific development briefs to guide developers;

ii   consider how the process of preparing community strategies can help identify needs and achieve consensus on delivery of housing provision appropriate to local needs;

iii   ensure that local housing need assessments are related to local conditions and are undertaken in a consistent manner, particularly in sub-regions where there is evidence of cross-boundary movements especially for journeys to work. Further advice on undertaking such assessments is provided in *Local Housing Needs Assessment: A Guide to Good Practice* (DETR, 2000);

iv   work closely with the Housing Corporation, registered social landlords, other housing providers, developers and new and local businesses, to secure sufficient affordable housing. Circulars 6/98 *(Planning and Affordable Housing)* and 1/97 *(Planning Obligations)* provide further guidance;

v   establish mechanisms to ensure that both low cost market and subsidised housing for rent are kept affordable in perpetuity, possibly through partnership with registered social landlords and through the use of legal agreements;

vi   work in partnership with local employers including those about to move to an area, to establish the scope for assistance to their employees to secure housing in the locality. The introduction of schemes to allow key workers to take the first step onto the housing ladder should be considered to ensure a long term source of labour for all sectors of the employment market;

vii   consider whether there is a need to seek lower thresholds as set out in Circular 6/98 (i.e. down to developments of 15 dwellings in urban areas). Where local authorities can demonstrate that local circumstances, particularly the likely viability of developments, justify adopting a lower threshold, they should bring forward proposals through the development plan process;

viii   consider how they might use the exercise of an urban capacity study to help identify opportunities for increasing affordable housing provision. Options may include, for example, sub-dividing existing properties, conversions from other uses or identifying suitable empty properties or unfit houses in need of repair;

ix   produce an empty homes strategy, identifying suitable vacant properties for affordable housing. The re-use of vacant properties can help make better use of urban capacity and reduce the demand for new build housing in the longer term; and

x   monitor the provision of affordable housing against their local target, and regularly review both the targets and the housing strategy to meet it. This may lead to revisions to the appropriate development plan policies.

c   The Regional Planning Bodies should monitor the overall regional provision of affordable housing against a provisional indicator of 18,000 to 19,000 affordable homes a year in the ROSE area. This indicator should be reviewed in the light of the cumulative result of local need assessments.

Housing Provision on Previously Developed Land

8.16 The key to ensuring the required amount of housing in the Region is delivered in a sustainable way, will be through local planning authorities following the principles set out in PPG3 *(Housing)*. In particular, maximising the re-use of previously developed land and existing buildings. Some data on derelict land is being collected for the National Land Use Database. Land may become available for redevelopment as a consequence of organisational changes such as those in health provision or the defence sector. Furthermore, Government is expecting that local authorities will identify further opportunities for additional housing as a result of undertaking urban capacity studies. The Government believes that by 2008 at least 60% of housing development in ROSE should be provided on previously developed land and through conversions of existing buildings, and that efforts should be made to improve the urban (including suburban) and rural environment and economy by the investment that this represents. London already achieves over 80% of housing development on previously developed land and through conversions of existing buildings and the Secretary of State would expect this to continue in future.

Policy H5

Within the context of improving the quality of urban living, full use should be made of the opportunities for increasing housing development within urban areas. Local authorities in ROSE should adopt a sequential approach to the allocation of land for housing and seek to achieve at least 60% of all new housing development on previously developed sites and through the conversions of existing buildings.

a   Local authorities in preparing development plans should:

   i   carry out rigorous studies of urban capacity and potential, ensuring consistency across local authority boundaries within the same local housing market;

   ii   identify vacant, poorly used and underused land which is suitable for development, as well as that which could benefit from policies to encourage change of use (for example, the better use of land currently used for surface car parking, allocated for employment or formerly used for defence purposes);

   iii   where suitable vacant and underused property has been identified, make proposals for the more intensive use of such sites, including providing greater choice and environmental enhancement for existing residents and users;

   iv   make proposals for high quality intensive residential and mixed used development on land close to town centres and at points of good public transport accessibility, or where public transport services can be improved as part of a planned approach (see chapter 5); and

   v   base policies for the release and development of land on a sequential approach as set out in PPG3 *(Housing)*.

b   Regional Planning Bodies and the Mayor of London should co-ordinate the programme of urban capacity studies undertaken by the local authorities and maintain consistency of approach by agreeing the standards to be applied.

c   In addition:

   i   Regional Development Agencies in liaison with central and local government should consider devising mechanisms for bringing forward small and fragmented areas of land for redevelopment, especially for affordable housing;

ii compulsory purchase orders can provide a useful tool in the assembly of sites for redevelopment; and

iii the National Land Use Database can provide information about derelict land. Using this and other information sources, local authorities, the Environment Agency, Regional Development Agencies and other partners need to collaborate in assessing the presence, condition and availability of vacant and poorly used land in order to formulate effective redevelopment proposals.

Chapter 9

Regional Transport Strategy

9.1   The geography of the South East creates a number of specific transport problems and opportunities. As the largest Region in the UK with a generally prosperous economy, close to neighbouring European countries, the impacts of high car use, through traffic and congestion are significant. At the same time the Region enjoys the benefits of proximity to wider markets. The Region's role as gateway to the rest of Europe and its internationally significant transport infrastructure is described in chapter 2 of this guidance. The influence of London is substantial and means that in general the Region's transport routes to London are well developed while orbital routes are less so.

9.2   The commitment to the key themes of this regional guidance - promoting urban renaissance, economy in the use of land, integrating land use and transport and rural development - will have significant implications for transport planning. Decisions relating to the spatial distribution of land uses, and the mix of land uses and design need to underpin and, wherever possible, enhance the viability of public transport. While local circumstances will influence what is possible, it is no longer acceptable to work on the premise that the car will represent the only realistic means of access. Delivery of this commitment will require a high quality, integrated transport system. This chapter sets out the Regional Transport Strategy (RTS) for the SERPLAN area. It provides the basis for further development of the RTS for the South East and the East of England. Furthermore, in London, the Mayor's Transport Strategy must have regard to this RTS.

9.3   Many of the measures required to support the RPG policy framework are likely to be capable of being addressed through Local Transport Plans (LTPs) or, in the case of London, through the Mayor's Transport Strategy and the Local Implementation Plans (LIPs) prepared by the London Borough Councils and subject to the Mayor's approval. Guidance on LTPs set out in this chapter should be reflected, where applicable, in the Mayor's Transport Strategy and LIPs. In addition, and notwithstanding the commitment to concentrate development, there is a need for investment to take place in both the inter-urban and inter-regional networks and facilities serving the Region. *Transport 2010 - The Ten Year Plan*, (DETR July 2000), is expected to deliver £180 billion of private and public funding nationally over the next ten years of which local transport is expected to account for £59 billion, including £19.3 billion allocated through LTPs.

Integrated Local Transport Plans have now replaced the scheme-by-scheme approach under which resources were allocated for new local transport projects. They will offer a major improvement over the previous arrangements by:

- covering five-year periods, offering greater certainty of future funding for local authorities;

- providing a strategic transport planning framework, linked to local development plans and regeneration proposals;

- covering both capital and revenue spending;

- giving local authorities more say in the allocation of capital resources;

- taking a partnership approach, involving local communities, local business and transport providers;

- placing greater emphasis on targets, performance indicators and monitoring; and

- emphasising integrated solutions looking across all types of transport.

Source: DETR, 2000. Transport 2010 – The Ten Year Plan

Policy T1

Policies should be developed which minimise the distance which people need to travel whilst enhancing choice and ease of access to activities, taking into account the needs of all users including disabled people and others with reduced mobility.

a   Development plans and/or local transport plans should:

   i   include transport policies and proposals which support delivery of urban renaissance, sustainable growth, regeneration and economy in the use of land;

   ii have regard to the following transport based locational criteria in developing land use strategies and making land use allocations which are consistent with the overall spatial, social, economic and environmental strategy for the region:

- development should be planned holistically to minimise the need for movement and to facilitate and encourage safe movement on foot, by cycle and public transport;

- development that generates a large number of passenger movements (e.g. cultural facilities or places of employment) should be located at or close to sites which provide, or have the potential to provide, ready and convenient access on foot, by cycle and public transport;

- development that generates a large quantity of freight and goods movements should be located at or close to sites which maximise the opportunity for carriage by rail, sea or inland waterway;

- development should be planned in such a way as to make best use of existing transportation networks and have regard to strategic priorities; and

- development should be planned to enhance the viability of new and existing public transport services;

iii give appropriate weight to environmental considerations, and in particular how the inter-relationship between land use and transportation planning can minimise the overall environmental impact; and

iv recognise the transport needs and character of the countryside. Rural transport policies and proposals need to be consistent with wider aims for rural development, particularly encouraging sustainable development and overcoming social exclusion and isolation.

b In addition, local authorities should:

i aim to achieve a measurable modal shift in favour of non-car modes of travel, particularly in urban areas, and as part of their local transport planning process, they should consider the development of appropriate targets including local traffic reduction targets;

ii work together with the Strategic Rail Authority, Highways Agency, public transport operators, the Regional Development Agencies and other relevant partners in preparing and implementing measures through the LTP and other investment programmes, both to improve management of the highway network and encourage greater use of non-car modes of travel. Further guidance on different elements of an integrated transport system, including parking provision and walking and cycling, is provided in the remainder of this chapter;

iii have regard to the regional spatial strategy set out in this guidance, as well as the investment strategy applicable in adjoining local authorities, in identifying future investment requirements; and

iv consider the potential role that road user charging and workplace parking levies may have as a means of addressing congestion particularly in 'hotspots' within the Western Policy Area (referred to in chapters 4 and 7). In bringing forward such proposals authorities will need to weigh carefully the costs and benefits in social, environmental and economic terms.

Travel Awareness and Travel Plans

9.4 Travel awareness campaigns can increase public recognition that there is a need to reduce the environmental impacts of car use. They can assist the process of introducing new measures, whether voluntary or through regulation or charging. They provide opportunities to inform individuals and organisations of measures which help widen the choices available to them in meeting a travel need.

9.5 Local authorities can play a major role in engaging the public, business community, health sector, education sector and transport industry in a meaningful partnership which promotes the development and implementation of Travel Plans. Travel Plans provide the framework for an organisation to optimise its use of transport, through the development and promotion of wider choice in travel modes and travel substitution. They are applicable in managing travel movement associated with existing patterns of development, as well as supporting new development proposals. For example, consultation is needed between the National Health Service and local authorities to prepare Travel Plans for hospitals which take into account the extent of the catchment areas, the 24 hour operation of many NHS facilities, and issues such as personal security of staff.

9.6 Travel Plans can contribute to the delivery of sustainable transport objectives by encouraging:

• reductions in congestion and pollution through reduced car use;

- reductions in the level of car parking required to support existing and additional land use proposals;

- increased use of walking, cycling and public transport;

- reduced traffic speeds and improved safety particularly for pedestrians and cyclists; and

- more environmentally friendly delivery and freight movements, including home delivery services.

9.7   Travel Plans can be seen as a positive measure in support of economic activity and growth in the South East. In particular they are likely to have an important role within economically buoyant areas such as the Western Policy Area where the promotion of wider choice and travel substitution can assist continued economic growth. Further advice on the implementation of Travel Plans can be found in the following Government Publications: *The Benefits of Green Transport Plans, A Travel Plan Resource Pack for Employers* and specifically for schools, *School Travel Strategies and Plans – A Best Practice Guide for Local Authorities* (DETR, 1999) as well as a *School Travel Resource Pack*.

Policy T2

Local authorities, working with partners including the public, the business community, educational establishments, the health authorities and the transport industry, should develop travel awareness strategies designed to encourage a change in travel habits which complements and is consistent with the proposed land use strategy. As part of this the local authority should encourage the development of Travel Plans for all major travel generating activities, both existing and proposed.

a   Development plans and/or local transport plans should:

    i   have regard to the potential contribution of a travel awareness strategy towards delivery of the overall objectives of the plans;

    ii   identify major travel generating activities within the plan area for which Travel Plans should be developed;

    iii   require planning applications for developments that will have significant transport implications, to include transport assessments in line with advice in Draft PPG13 *(Transport)* and provide proposals for a Travel Plan; and

    iv   set targets for the adoption of Travel Plans within the plan area.

b   In addition:

    i   in determining land use allocations within development plans, local authorities should take into account the positive role that Travel Plans can have in terms of achieving a more sustainable pattern of movement. However, unacceptable or poorly located development should never be permitted because of the existence of a Travel Plan;

    ii   in identifying major travel generating activities, local authorities should take into account the cumulative effect that may arise from a series of small scale proposals. In such circumstances, local authorities should encourage, through their policies and their LTPs, the development of an area-wide framework which enables the benefits of Travel Plans to be applied across a number of individual activities or organisations; and

iii local authorities should ensure that they have in place a regime for monitoring the effectiveness of Travel Plans.

Parking Strategy and Maximum Parking Standards

9.8   The overall approach on parking needs to complement and reinforce the spatial strategy set out in this guidance. In particular it needs to support the commitment to urban renaissance whereby development is concentrated in locations which are highly accessible, or have the potential to be highly accessible, by non-car modes.

9.9   Local authorities are advised to include, as part of their LTP proposals for managing demand, details of a comprehensive parking strategy which co-ordinates their policies on parking standards with those on parking provision, controls, charges and enforcement. In doing so they need to consider the potential for using revenues from future workplace parking levies and congestion charging schemes in support of investment in transport infrastructure. Where local authorities and private companies operate public on- and off-street car parks, their supply and pricing policies can influence commuter parking and help to encourage the use of public transport.

9.10 As alternative modes of travel are developed, consideration needs to be given to the introduction of increasing levies for the use of parking provision at places of work. Those areas in which access by non-car modes provides a convenient and ready alternative, or where car based travel has an adverse impact on the quality of life and the environment, will be expected to consider the early introduction of levies for workplace parking as part of the local transport planning process. In considering parking provision attention needs to be paid to safety issues and also to the mobility needs of people with disabilities who rely on the private car for independent mobility. Designated parking for disabled motorists needs to be provided.

9.11 It is essential that there is a consistent approach to the determination of parking standards across the Region to avoid the destructive potential for competitive provision of parking between different locations to the detriment of sustainable development. The context for setting parking standards in the South East is set out in Draft PPG13 *(Transport)*. This requires development plans to set maximum levels of parking for broad classes of development to encourage sustainable transport choices and promote development in locations which are well served by public transport, walking and cycling. Draft PPG13 *(Transport)* encourages the adoption of more rigorous parking standards where this is considered appropriate. The South East Region exhibits a wide range of social and economic circumstances which necessitates a flexible approach to standard setting at a local level. There are, however, a number of areas within ROSE where it will be appropriate to apply parking standards that are tighter than the standards proposed in Draft PPG13 *(Transport)*. Parking standards for the ROSE area must be complementary to and consistent with those for outer London.

9.12 The Secretary of State considers that as a base-line, the maximum car parking standard for development within the scope of the Use Class B1 of the Town and Country Planning (Use Class) Order 1988 and in the ROSE area, particularly in urban areas, should be within the range 1:30 – 1:100 parking spaces per m^2 of gross floorspace. Guidance on maximum parking standards for London is currently set out in RPG3. The Mayor of London will want to review parking standards in London in preparing the Spatial Development and Transport Strategies, having regard to this guidance and to Draft PPG13 *(Transport)*. As an interim measure, in the light of experience and in order to achieve greater consistency with the ROSE area, the Secretary of State hereby modifies the guidance on car parking standards in RPG3, to broaden the range of acceptable parking standards for employment generating development in outer London from 1:300 – 1:600 per m^2 to 1:100 – 1:600 per m^2 of floor space.

9.13   Guidance on the level of parking provision appropriate for housing development is set out in PPG3. The concentration of development and emphasis on urban renewal should make public transport more viable and create the opportunity to reduce further the need for parking in urban areas.

9.14   The standards set out in Draft PPG13 *(Transport)* do not apply to development proposals below the relevant thresholds. Local planning authorities are advised to adopt maximum standards for parking at small developments, but may use their discretion in setting detailed levels, so as to reflect local circumstances. By virtue of the thresholds, this locally-based approach will cover most development in rural areas.

Policy T3

Local authorities should, in consultation with adjoining authorities, adopt maximum parking standards for all new development proposals.

a   Development plans and/or local transport plans in ROSE should:

    i   include restraint based maximum parking standards in line with advice in Draft PPG13 *(Transport)*;

    ii   set as a base-line a maximum parking standard for B1 land use within the range 1:30m^2 and 1:100m^2;

    iii   identify the basis for and justification for the maximum parking standard for B1 land use; and

    iv   include maximum parking standards for residential development which are more rigorous than those set out in national planning guidance (PPG3) where this is necessary in support of urban renaissance.

b   In setting their maximum parking standard for B1 land use local authorities in ROSE should take into consideration the following factors:

    i   relationship with adjoining authorities – authorities should take into consideration the context set by the standards adopted in adjoining and competing areas and the spatial and physical relationship between adjoining urban areas. Authorities adjoining the outer London Boroughs, or who have a strong spatial or economic relationship with London would normally be expected to adopt as a base-line a maximum parking standard at, or close to, that which applies in the outer London Boroughs. Authorities should consider imposing a more rigorous standard than 1:100m^2 in areas whose character and levels of accessibility are similar to those in outer London or where the spatial distribution of development has the potential to encourage and support a viable public transport system;

    ii   level of activity – in those parts of the Region where traffic congestion is a key concern, authorities should consider the role that more rigorous parking standards might play as part of an integrated transport system. In those areas of the Region which are currently less economically successful careful consideration may need to be given as to the impact that a more rigorous parking standard may have on the prospects of achieving economic regeneration. Authorities in such areas will need to balance carefully the issues associated with managing congestion, promoting wider choice in travel mode and realising economic growth in determining the appropriate maximum parking standard. This may require authorities to adopt a phased approach to the provision of parking whereby parking provision is reduced over time as economic growth occurs and public transport accessibility is improved; and

iii size of settlement – larger urban areas are more likely to be capable of supporting an attractive and viable public transport service. Local authorities should take into consideration the likely level and availability of public transport in determining the appropriate maximum parking standard. In particular they should consider opportunities which emerge through the spatial strategy for planned growth to optimise the potential for public transport. Areas which already or potentially have a high level of public transport accessibility would normally be expected to adopt more rigorous parking standards.

c   In setting and reviewing their maximum car parking standards in outer London, local authorities should note that the Secretary of State hereby modifies RPG3 in the following respect: in table 6.1 (page 74) of RPG3, the range of off-street parking spaces for employment generating development in outer London is broadened from 1:300 – 1:600 per m² to 1:100 – 1:600 per m² of floorspace. The guidance in RPG3 on standards for inner London and central London remains unchanged.

d   For land uses other than B1, local authorities should refer to guidance in Draft PPG13 *(Transport)* and in doing so they should consider adopting a similar approach to that outlined for B1 in this guidance. Local authorities should be mindful of the need to ensure that in adopting more rigorous maximum parking standards they do not create perverse incentives which encourage development to be located away from town centres or that threaten future levels of investment in town centres.

e   In addition, local authorities should co-ordinate their policies on parking standards with those on parking provision, controls, charges and enforcement, through the preparation of a comprehensive car parking strategy as part of their LTP proposals for managing demand. Such strategies should support a more integrated transport system (for example, managing parking provision at public transport interchanges) and encourage co-operation with businesses and the development sector to seek to reduce parking provision at existing development and manage commercial activities in ways which reduce the length and number of generated movements (both passenger and freight).

Walking and Cycling

9.15 Walking and cycling are the ideal forms of travel for many shorter journeys both in urban and rural areas. They provide the most environmentally-friendly and healthiest ways of travelling. To encourage their use for travel to work, school, shopping and other purposes, a range of improvements needs to be made to the design of the built environment and the provision of infrastructure. For example, adequately signalled crossing points are needed at difficult road junctions and facilities for cyclists need to be provided such as secure cycle storage at places of work, schools, railway stations and recreational and leisure facilities.

9.16 The National Cycling Strategy, endorsed by the Government, provides a framework for co-operation between government, business and the voluntary sector to improve the role of cycling in the future. The South East is particularly prone to congestion and cycling can play a significant role in its planning strategies. However, many areas currently have cycle mode shares significantly below the national average.

9.17 PPG13 *(Transport)* advises that local authorities should use their planning and transport powers to also give greater priority to walking. Further advice is available in other Government publications, such as *Encouraging Walking: Advice for Local Authorities* (DETR, 2000). Guidance on *Full Local Transport Plans* (DETR, March 2000), requires authorities to prepare separate local cycle and walking strategies, the main elements of which should be incorporated in their LTPs. These strategies should recognise the important role that walking and cycling can make as part of an integrated transport system, as well as their value for leisure and recreation. Other organisations have also prepared practical advice, for example, *A Safer Journey to School* (Transport 2000, 1999).

Policy T4

Walking and cycling should be vigorously promoted especially for shorter distances, as the healthiest and most environmentally-friendly ways to travel.

a   Development plans and/or local transport plans should:

    i   encourage the extent and safety of walking and cycling in both urban and rural areas;

    ii   include policies and proposals for safe, direct, convenient and continuous local networks of pedestrian and cycle routes which link the main land uses including schools, hospitals and cultural facilities;

    iii   require new development to make adequate provision for pedestrians and cyclists, including measures to link development with existing footpaths and cycle networks, to provide new links where appropriate and to provide for adequate, secure and convenient storage of cycles and facilities for cyclists;

    iv   plan development in urban areas, including the siting of local services and public transport routes, and street patterns, so as to facilitate walking as a primary travel mode for trips between home and local services or to access public transport; and

    v   include policies which aim to improve upon the central target in the National Cycling Strategy of increasing the number of cycle trips to four times its 1996 level by 2012.

b   In addition, local authorities should:

    i   ensure that all relevant aspects of their LTPs (including road safety, planning and social policies) reinforce policies to promote walking and cycling to achieve the goal of safe and sustainable transport. Safety issues are very important and pedestrian and cycle networks should include safe road junction crossings where appropriate;

    ii   work with partners to carry out improvements to walking and cycle networks and facilities which enhance their directness, convenience, safety and amenity. In doing so they should look at ways in which local cycling and walking networks can be linked into regional and national routes. They should also consider the opportunity to re-allocate road space in favour of pedestrians and cyclists. Walking and cycling networks should be expanded, in the process focusing them more on the needs of local communities and utilising the resources of other bodies. In doing so, authorities should work with the development industry to promote street patterns which support this aim;

    iii   work with transport providers and local business (using, for example, development control powers) to secure improved facilities for cyclists both at work and on passenger transport; and

    iv   ensure that cycle networks and routes are developed strategically, which may mean groups of authorities working together to ensure connections across administrative boundaries.

Public Transport

9.18 Delivery of the overall strategy requires local authorities to encourage a greater proportion of journeys to be made by public transport. Particular attention needs to be given to ensuring that the inter-urban strategic public transport network provides for linkages with adjacent regions, and to airports, seaports and the Channel Tunnel. To achieve this, the range of services provided by public transport and the quality of the experience need to be significantly improved to make it a more acceptable option for the travelling public. Relevant factors are notably reliability, frequency, cost, travel time, comfort, cleanliness, safety, evening and weekend provision, information and co-ordination between services.

Policy T5

Public transport (bus, train and water-borne) should be improved to enable it to compete more effectively with the private car and to increase its share of total travel.

a Development plans and/or local transport plans should:

   i identify those elements of the strategic inter-urban public transport network which lie within the plan area;

   ii include policies to protect facilities which support the use and development of the inter-urban and urban public transport networks;

   iii include proposals to develop the inter-urban, urban and rural public transport network, including the development of inter-modal interchange facilities, such that it supports the spatial strategy and the locational policies set out in this guidance (for example, locating higher trip generating development close to public transport services);

   iv include policies which ensure that where a disused rail line or railway land may have the reasonable prospect of re-use for transport purposes in the foreseeable future, it is not severed by new development; and

   v identify a strategy which secures attractive and reliable bus services in support of the spatial strategy. Consideration should be given to the potential for encouraging bus services through reallocation and priority use of road space, particularly where the spatial distribution of land uses is such as to have the potential to encourage and support a viable public transport system.

b In addition:

   i local authorities, the Strategic Rail Authority, public transport operators and adjoining authorities should work together in identifying, prioritising and securing investment in support of the Region's strategic inter-urban public transport network, including roadside real-time information facilities;

   ii proposals should be developed which improve the facilities for convenient and accessible interchange between the strategic inter-urban public transport network, local public transport and other modes;

   iii local authorities should identify in their LTPs minimum standards of service for key interchange locations and identify in conjunction with all the relevant partners investment proposals which address any deficiency;

   iv local authorities and public transport operators, should work together to pursue opportunities to secure and promote integrated networks of high quality local bus services and other public transport services that complement the Region's inter-urban public transport network; and

LTPs should also include a strategy for improving travel choice in rural areas. Funding sources for rural initiatives include the Rural Transport Development Fund, the Rural Transport Partnership Scheme, the Rural Bus Subsidy Grant and the Rural Bus Challenge.

Freight

9.19 An efficient and effective freight distribution system is vital to the economy. However, freight distribution should not be at the expense of the wider community and the environment. It must be sustainable. Key aims for the freight distribution industry are:

- to improve the efficiency of distribution so that it contributes to steady economic growth in a sustainable manner;

- to make better use of transport infrastructure through better forward planning;

- to reduce the environmental impact of freight distribution;

- to increase the proportion of freight moved by rail, inland waterways and coastal shipping; and

- to manage development pressures through better forward planning to minimise environmental impact and loss of habitats.

9.20 It is recognised that road freight will continue to predominate and as such strategies will need to be developed, in partnership with local authorities, the industry, local communities and the Highways Agency, to reduce its environmental impact and increase its efficiency. Account will need to be taken of the aspirations and views of the Strategic Rail Authority on developing the rail network as part of an integrated transport system. In order to realise the potential of the rail network for freight haulage, enhancements of both the track and gauge are likely to be required. The identification and development of inter-modal interchange facilities may help to realise the potential of the rail, inland waterway and coastal shipping networks for the movement of freight.

Policy T6

A fully integrated freight distribution system should be promoted which makes the most efficient and effective use of road, rail, inland waterways and coastal shipping.

a   In taking forward this Regional Transport Strategy, the Regional Planning Bodies and Mayor of London, working with the Strategic Rail Authority, Highway Agency, port authorities and other partners, should:

i   identify a strategic freight network which supports the overall strategy and which promotes the efficient and effective use of road, rail, inland waterways and coastal shipping networks; and

ii   include a criteria based assessment framework which will allow individual authorities to respond to proposals for inter-modal interchange facilities on a consistent basis.

b   Development plans and/or local transport plans should:

i   identify those elements of a strategic freight network which lie within the plan area in order to channel appropriate movements to it;

ii   include policies which support making the best use of all existing infrastructure in support of the efficient movement and timely delivery of goods while at the same time reducing its environmental impact;

iii include policies designed to increase the proportion of freight moved by rail, inland waterways and coastal shipping, for example by protecting existing facilities or by maximising the potential of development sites to enhance access to rail and inland waterways for the movement of freight;

iv include proposals to safeguard sites for rail freight facilities, including wharves and ports and permit development for rail and water freight operations and associated facilities for modal transfer where these would assist in the development of the strategic freight network;

v include economically viable proposals for the development of inter-modal interchange facilities where they support the overall strategy, subject to a satisfactory appraisal; and

vi support the spatial strategy and locational policies set out in this guidance, for example, for development with higher generation of freight and commercial traffic to be located closest to inter-modal freight facilities, rail freight facilities, port and wharves or roads designed and managed as traffic distributors.

c In addition:

i consideration should be given to the potential contribution that Freight Quality Partnerships could make to the development of a strategic multi-modal freight network;

ii road improvements and commercial vehicle priority measures need to be considered as part of a comprehensive approach to freight distribution. Such measures may help speed the flow of goods and services as well as improving access to the rail, inland waterways and coastal shipping networks; and

iii local authorities, port authorities and adjoining authorities should work with the Strategic Rail Authority and the Highways Agency to enhance the level of rail freight access to ports and to develop combined transport freight systems and fully integrated distribution systems.

Improving Seaport Facilities

9.21 Ports are a vital link in the supply chain to and from the Region's trading partners and need to be integrated with wider transport networks. The 1998 White Paper *A New Deal for Transport: Better for Everyone* gave four key aims for the Government's policy on ports:

- to promote UK and regional competitiveness by encouraging reliable and efficient distribution and access to markets;

- to enhance environmental and operational performance by encouraging the provision of multi-modal access to markets;

- to make the best use of existing infrastructure, in preference to expansion wherever practicable; and

- to promote best environmental standards in the design and operation of ports including where new development is justified.

The Government's ports policy paper will develop these aims.

9.22 The reliable and efficient distribution of goods depends in part upon a vigorous ports industry. Fair competition between ports is healthy and the Government's policy – both for the UK and EU – is to avoid distorting that competition. In order to ensure that this policy is delivered it is important that a strategic and regional view of the ports sector is provided.

9.23 The ports industry has changed substantially over the last 30 years and this has increased the importance of some South East ports and changed the role of others. The emergence of the European Union as a principal trading market, the growth of a global trading economy, increases in ship sizes (particularly the drafts of deep sea container ships) and modal shift (including the use of boxes, trailers and maritime containers) have all had an impact on the relative importance of the ports in the South East. In addition, the opening of the Channel Tunnel has had a major impact on the importance of certain ferry ports. It has brought new choice and competition to ferry services on the short-sea Channel crossing. As a consequence several ports competing in this market have lost ferry services.

9.24 These changes in the ports industry have served to give us a pattern of regionally significant ports in the South East. These include London, Thamesport, Southampton, Medway Ports (including Sheerness), Dover, Portsmouth and Harwich.

Policy T7

The sustainable development of seaports and port facilities (including road and rail access to them) should be supported for international deep sea, short sea and coastal shipping.

a   Development plans and/or local transport plans should identify and safeguard from other development:

   i   land for interchange facilities and access improvements to ports especially to promote the use of rail freight and inland waterways; and

   ii   appropriate sites of port and wharf use that will be required to meet changing market needs.

b   In addition, local authorities, port authorities, the shipping industry and other interested parties should work in partnership to produce development strategies for port facilities and access to them, which are sustainable and make best use of existing facilities. In developing their strategies they should:

   i   have regard to the potential for, and plan to encourage, growth in traffic to be accommodated by rail and inland waterways with the aim of optimising their mode share;

   ii   work with transport providers and other authorities whose areas include ports serving similar markets;

   iii   carefully consider the benefit of continued port operations within the wider spatial strategy in determining the future role of ports. In particular, consideration should be given to identifying the land use which maximises the contribution of a particular site to delivery of the economic, social and environmental objectives of the overall strategy;

   iv   have regard to the economic and environmental potential of the river and river front and the need to avoid the loss of waterfront to development which would not benefit significantly from a riverside location; and

   v   take account of the needs for port development, regeneration and leisure access to river and coastal frontage.

c   A study of the port and shipping markets is required in order to develop a more regionally specific ports strategy. It will need to acknowledge the role of neighbouring ports in adjoining regions, and inform the next revision of the RPGs for the South East and East of England and the Spatial Development Strategy for London.

Airports

9.25 The Government's policy on UK airports is being developed. The background is set out in the 1985 White Paper: *Airports Policy*. The 1998 White Paper *A New Deal For Transport: Better for Everyone* announced the Government's intention to take a strategic view of UK airports policy looking some 30 years ahead and to develop this within the framework of the Government's sustainable development principles. In March 1999 the Government further announced the setting up of a study to look at airports in the South East and East of England. This will culminate in a White Paper which will take into account the results of that study (and those of other regional airport studies announced in the 1998 White Paper), and the outcome of the Heathrow Terminal 5 inquiry. This guidance will need to be re-examined following that work in order to include a strategic steer on the role and future development of airports in the South East in the light of that national policy.

9.26 Airports have become major transport interchanges and traffic generators, and attract a range of related and non-related developments. This raises issues about the extent to which planned development is related to the operation of the airport, and is sustainable given the prevailing and planned levels, and the potential for enhancement, of public transport. A key issue concerns the modes of surface access to airports; these need to be sustainable and should be planned as part of the wider transport strategy for the local area.

Policy T8

Any surface access measures necessary to cater for airport growth either within existing planned limits or for further expansion, should be sustainable. Any further development associated with such airport growth should also be sustainable in nature.

a   Development plans and/or local transport plans should:

   i   ensure that any development of airport surface access takes account of the wider transport strategy for the local area and provides for a wider choice of mode of travel;

   ii   identify and safeguard land for access improvements to airports, especially for public transport modes; and

   iii   consider the extent to which development is related to the operation of the airport and is sustainable given the prevailing levels, and potential for enhancement of public transport, cycling and walking.

b   In addition, airport operators should be partners (through Airport Transport Fora where they exist) in implementing surface transport initiatives to ensure that access by public transport is enhanced. This may involve, for example, parking restraint and development of a Travel Plan for the airport, covering journeys by employees and users of the airport.

Investment in Regional Transport

9.27 *Transport 2010 – The Ten Year Plan* sets out the Government's plans for greatly increased public and private funding expected to provide £180 billion nationally in the ten years from April 2001. This includes £121 billion of public and private capital investment, an increase of almost 75% in real terms compared with the proceeding 10 years. One of the functions of the RTS is to identify regional priorities for that investment reflecting the priorities of The Ten Year Plan as well as supporting the regional spatial strategy set out in this guidance.

9.28 It is acknowledged that the RTS set out within this guidance will need to be developed in more detail in subsequent revisions, principally in response to developing Government policies and the outcome of relevant studies. Notwithstanding the need to develop the RTS in more detail, it is clear that investment proposals will need to deliver a high quality integrated sustainable transport system. Priorities for investment in transport infrastructure will be expected to:

- serve the Region's role as the transport gateway to the continent;

- improve the regional transport links between the Thames Gateway, Priority Areas for Economic Regeneration, other major urban areas, ports, airports and the Channel Tunnel Rail Link; and

- facilitate access to the potential growth areas.

Policy T9

The regional programme of transport investment in support of the spatial strategy set out within this Regional Transport Strategy, should be developed and reviewed.

a   Development plans should include policies which safeguard delivery of:

    i   the specific investment proposals identified in this guidance (subject to the special arrangements in London, set out below); and

    ii   other major proposals where they are consistent with the spatial strategy and the regional priorities for investment in transport infrastructure.

b   Implementation of the investment proposals included in this guidance, should be progressed at the earliest possible opportunity, subject to satisfactory appraisal, consultation with the Mayor of London as appropriate, the completion of all statutory processes and the availability of finance.

c   In addition:

    i   Regional Planning Bodies, local authorities, the Strategic Rail Authority, public transport operators, the development industry and other partners need to work together in developing proposals which are consistent with the spatial strategy, regional priorities for investment in transport infrastructure and the investment strategies of each party;

    ii   the Regional Planning Body for the East of England will need to consider the priorities set out here as they affect Bedfordshire, Essex and Hertfordshire in conjunction with those identified in RPG6 for East Anglia, and form a view on the priorities for the East of England as a whole; and

    iii   in London the Mayor is responsible for producing a transport strategy, having regard to national policy and regional guidance.

i   Priority Improvements to the Public Transport and Rail Network

9.29   Improvements to the network of public transport services are necessary in order to support the spatial strategy set out in chapter 4 of this guidance. Proposals which are considered to be of regional significance include:

    i   Channel Tunnel Rail Link (including Phase 2) – a priority in the context of the Region's role as a transport gateway and in support of the development of Thames Gateway;

    ii   Thameslink 2000 – a major proposal in the context of improving regional transport links;

    iii   delivery of a sustainable pattern of development within the Kent Thames-side area of the Thames Gateway will need to be supported by a proposal for a major improvement to the public transport system within Kent Thames-side if a more sustainable pattern of movement is to be achieved;

iv   an East West Rail Link through London such as Cross Rail;

v   modernisation of the West Coast Main Line and upgrading of the East Coast Main Line to facilitate increases in the frequencies and speeds of trains between London and the Midlands and the North;

vi   delivery of a sustainable pattern of development within the South Hampshire conurbation will need to be supported by measures which will support a more sustainable pattern of movement. It is likely that this will include a proposal for a major improvement to the public transport system in the area between Southampton and Portsmouth, such as the South Hampshire Rapid Transport System;

vii enhancement of east-west public transport links north of London such as the proposed East West Rail Link;

viii improved rail links to Heathrow from the west such as Airtrack;

ix   further rail capacity enhancements e.g. London-Brighton line; and

x   gauge and capacity enhancements on freight routes to major ports such as to the Channel Tunnel.

9.30 In addition other priorities for investment will include:

i   local public transport schemes identified as priorities by local authorities and being taken forward within the Region's Local Transport Plans; and

ii   those priorities in London established through the Mayor's transport strategy and Local Implementation Plans.

ii   Priority Improvements to the Strategic Road Network

9.31 *A New Deal for Trunk Roads* published in June 1998 identified a core network of Trunk Roads which are of strategic importance. Major improvements on the core network within the South East will in future be brought forward as part of the development of the RTS. As part of the *New Deal for Trunk Roads* a programme of investment in the core network was identified which addressed the most immediate problems – the Targeted Programme of Improvements. Delivery of these schemes is consistent with the regional priorities for investment in transport infrastructure and will support delivery of the spatial strategy.

9.32 The start date for those schemes where all the statutory procedures have been completed is as follows:

A27 Polegate Bypass	2000/01
A41 Aston Clinton Bypass	2000/01
A43 M40-B4031 Improvement	2000/01
A6 Clapham Bypass	2000/01
A10 Wadesmill Bypass	2001/02
A120 Stansted-Braintree	2001/02
A21 Lamberhurst Bypass	2001/02
M25 Junctions 12-15 Widening	2002/03

9.33 A planned start of works for the remaining schemes in the programme is expected by 2005, subject to the completion of all necessary statutory procedures:

A421 Great Barford Bypass

A34 Chieveley/M4 Junction 13 Improvement

A249 Iwade-Queenborough Improvement

A2 Bean-Cobham Widening Phase 1

A2 Bean-Cobham Widening Phase 2

A2/A282 Dartford Improvement

The A23 Coulsdon Relief Road, which appeared in *A New Deal for Trunk Roads*, is now a matter for the Mayor of London.

iii   Multi-Modal Studies

9.34 *A New Deal for Trunk Roads* set out a programme of studies which were initially identified in response to the need to address problems associated with the Trunk Road network. However, they will focus on identifying investment proposals which facilitate delivery of the spatial strategy and are consistent with the overall strategy. The following programme of studies have been identified for the South East:

Access to Hastings	Multi-Modal Study	started 1999/00
A3 Hindhead	Roads Based Study	started 1999/00
London Orbital	Multi-Modal Study	started 1999/00
London to South West & South Wales	Multi-Modal Study	started 1999/00
M27 South Hampshire	Integrated Transport Study	started 1999/00
A27 Worthing/Lancing	Integrated Transport Study	started 1999/00
South Coast Corridor (Southampton to Ramsgate)	Multi-Modal Study	commencing 2000/01
London to South Midlands	Multi-Modal Study	started 2000/01
London to Reading	Multi-Modal Study	commencing 2000/01
London to Ipswich	Multi-Modal Study	started 2000/01
A34 North of Southampton	Multi-Modal Study	commencing after 2001

9.35 The outcome of each study will be considered by the relevant Regional Planning Body or the Mayor of London where appropriate. Where the outcome of a study is consistent with the overall strategy of this guidance and the priorities for investment in transport infrastructure set out above, it is expected that proposals will be progressed at the earliest possible opportunity, subject to a satisfactory appraisal, the completion of all statutory processes, consultation with the Mayor as appropriate, and the availability of finance.

iv   Developing the Regional Transport Strategies and Proposed Further Studies

9.36 A priority for the development of the RTS should be the identification of key multi-modal routes, having regard to the spatial strategy and existing regional priorities for investment in transport infrastructure. Through this process specific proposals for future investment may emerge for inclusion as part of the RTS.

9.37 In addition to the studies already underway, a number of additional studies will be required. These will need to examine the capability of the existing transport infrastructure to facilitate and support delivery of the spatial strategy set out within this guidance. It is proposed that these additional studies should consider:

i improved rail links to the Channel Tunnel – rail links to the Channel Tunnel from both the wider South East and East Kent are in need of improvement. Consideration of the rail links between Hastings, Ashford and East Kent will be an issue that needs to be taken into account as part of the South Coast Corridor Multi-Modal Study;

ii improved transport links in the Thames Gateway - the role and benefits of additional multi-modal transport links in support of the objectives for the Thames Gateway area should be considered. Options could include an increase in cross river capacity east of Dartford (dependent upon work already underway as part of the London Orbital Study) and movement issues between London and Southend, as well as the impact of CTRL and possible increased use of river transport;

iii public transport services in the Western Policy Area – the size and proximity of settlements in the west and south west of the Region, where growth pressures are highest, have lead to diverse travel patterns being established, particularly for commuting and to a lesser extent for leisure and shopping. These movements are not well catered for by public transport and this has led to high levels of congestion on the inter-urban road network. Facilitating sustainable economic growth in this area will depend both on reducing car usage within the urban areas and an improved inter-urban public transport system. The work would need to be linked to the existing programme of studies, in particular the London Orbital and London to Reading Multi-Modal Studies; and

iv a study of the port and shipping markets – as detailed above at policy T7.

9.38 As part of the development of options for the potential growth areas the transport investment needs will also need to be considered both for travel within the relevant areas and to improve their external links. The lead times associated with the provision of transport infrastructure will need to be taken into account, particularly the longer lead times associated with the development of viable public transport services. Further guidance on the provision of infrastructure is provided in PPG12 (Development Plans) and the proposed studies of the potential growth areas are referred to in more detail in chapter 12 of this guidance.

Chapter 10

Supply and Development of Other Infrastructure - Water, Waste and Energy

10.1 Sustainable development in the Region also depends on how issues are addressed in relation to flooding, to the water cycle, to waste and to energy. All these have wider impacts on the global environment and on the resources of the Region. There are considerable pressures arising out of the demand for development on areas of flood plain, demand for domestic water and energy supplies and the management of waste. These are related to the size of the population and the scale of activity within the South East. Decreasing average household size also has implications for the relative efficiency in the use of water and energy, and the generation of waste. Most of the buildings and services in the South East are established and updating them with more energy and water efficient systems will require investment. Furthermore, the extent of land protected for its environmental, landscape or cultural value has implications for the location of new essential infrastructure. The relatively low rainfall in the South East and the effects of climate change on weather patterns and sea level are important considerations. Climate change and the scale and form of future development will affect the scale and nature of the demands placed on essential service infrastructure in the Region.

10.2 Demands for water and energy supplies and for land for disposal of waste could continue to increase significantly unless more sustainable alternative practices and development patterns can be achieved. There is a need to introduce new resource efficient practices and appliances and the development of new infrastructure as part of the urban development and renewal proposed by this guidance. The challenge for the South East is to find more sustainable approaches to infrastructure provision.

10.3 It is the Government's policy that consideration must be given to whether or not the existing infrastructure for water supply and quality, treatment and disposal of waste, and the provision of energy are sustainable in the longer term and how they might be modified. Wherever possible,

- resources should be conserved (resource conservation)

- demand for supplies should be managed (demand management)

- resources should be used as locally as possible (proximity principle)

- alternative options should be considered in order to identify the best practicable environmental option (BPEO).

Flooding

10.4 There are three kinds of major flood risk: fluvial (resulting from high flows in rivers), tidal (where high tides in river estuaries flood adjacent land) and coastal (resulting from tidal conditions and meteorological surge and prevailing wind conditions). Climate change is likely to exacerbate the risk of river flooding, and together with the steady lowering of land in the South East will increase the risk from tidal and coastal flooding. Flood plains have been identified across the region by the Environment Agency based on a 1% probability of exceedence per annum for rivers and a 0.5% probability of exceedence per annum for coastal flooding. More extreme but less likely floods will affect areas beyond the indicative flood plain and flooding may also occur almost anywhere when exceptionally heavy rainfall overwhelms the capacity of the drainage infrastructure.

10.5 All forms of flooding can cause widespread damage and risk to life, and over time a range of works have been carried out to reduce flood risk – most notably the Thames Barrier and associated river walls, which together protect the capital to a 0.1% probability of exceedence per annum standard. Most rivers and coastal areas in the Region have some form of managed defence to alleviate flood risk. However, river flood plains are part of the natural regime of rivers and valuable habitats depend on periodic flooding. A sustainable approach seeks to maintain their role as flood plains and ensure their continued contribution to biodiversity. The Region includes many areas, particularly close to the Thames, where there is already extensive building in flood plains. It is important that development here takes account of the risk of flooding and that undeveloped and undefended flood plains are protected from inappropriate development.

10.6 It would be unsustainable in the context of this Region to carry out flood defence schemes on rivers in order to free flood plains for development. There may be some scope for limited adjustments of levels at the edge of flood plains to enable development to take place without detriment to flood risk. In coastal areas, criteria are being developed by the Environment Agency and others for determining where it would be desirable to continue to maintain coastal defences against flooding and where it may be preferable to allow natural processes to take over. Shoreline Management Plans now exist for the whole of the South East coast. These make a valuable contribution to the understanding of coastal processes and towards the goal of achieving sustainable coastal defence and protection measures by informing the planning system.

10.7 A further concern is the need for a sustainable approach to run-off from redeveloped or newly built up sites and for the control of both rate and quality of discharge close to the source, in order to avoid adverse impacts on river regimes with a consequent risk of erosion, flooding and ecological damage. Various techniques, both old and new, are available. A number involve increased drainage by percolation into the ground. This reproduces natural drainage processes better than positive drainage direct to a watercourse, and provides a more acceptable way of eliminating pollutants than the use of gullies and interceptors, except on contaminated sites or those overlying vulnerable aquifers that require protection. Again, the need for costly upgrading of pipe networks may be avoided by the use of such techniques in conjunction with development and redevelopment in built up areas.

Policy INF1

Development should be guided away from areas at risk or likely to be at risk in future from flooding, or where it would increase the risk of flood damage elsewhere. Existing flood defences should be protected where they continue to be relevant.

a   Development plans should:

    i   include policies to protect flood plains and to protect land liable to tidal or coastal flooding from development, based on the Environment Agency's indicative maps, supplemented where necessary by historical and modelled flood data and indications as to other areas which could be at risk in future;

    ii   provide criteria for redevelopment proposals in river flood plains, in order to minimise their cumulative adverse impact and secure enhancement of the flood water storage and ecological role of flood plains;

    iii   take account of emerging thinking on the need for 'managed retreat' from selected coastal defences; and

    iv   encourage the adoption of sustainable urban drainage practices (see below).

b   In addition:

    i   the Environment Agency plays an important role in identifying the nature and extent of flood risk and in determining priorities for flood studies and the need for flood management measures. Measures may be identified in Local Environment Agency Plans (LEAPS); and

    ii   collaboration between a range of organisations in the preparation and implementation of Biodiversity Action Plans (BAPs) can also make a contribution, for example, in enhancing the role of rivers and flood plains as important wetland habitats for wildlife.

The Water Cycle - Supply and Quality

10.8   Water quality, water supply and drainage are closely interlinked, and affect the condition of both rivers and groundwater. There is a legacy in parts of the Region of over-abstraction, contamination affecting groundwater, and poor quality discharges to rivers, generally from sewage treatment works. These problems are being tackled, respectively, by:

- application of more rigorous standards in licensing abstractions;

- securing remediation of contaminated sites on redevelopment by treatment, containment or removal and by enforcement for which the Contaminated Land (England) Regulations 2000 will provide stronger powers; and

- enhancement of sewage works discharges through schemes agreed (with Government funds) under the Asset Management Process.

The problem specific to London of storm water overflows from combined sewers is currently dealt with using the Thames Bubbler mobile oxygenating plant, but long term solutions are required.

10.9   Water issues potentially pose certain limits to growth in particular areas. In particular, water abstraction has to be limited to avoid low river flows and steady depletion of groundwater aquifers; and the capacity of sewage treatment plant is limited by the dilution available at the receiving watercourse since the natural processes that clean up the river cease to operate when effluent concentration is too high. Where these limits are encountered, the problem may be overcome only by very costly measures such as pumping over significant distances, which may also be seen as unsustainable, and plans should therefore identify such problems and seek to promote alternative patterns of development.

10.10   Historically the South East has been one of the driest parts of the country and demands on water resources are already critical in parts of the Region. The need to balance the growing demand for water with the needs of the environment is crucial. Even where there is theoretical capacity, timely investment in infrastructure is required to ensure that new development does not adversely affect water supplies or water quality. These issues require early identification in studies on location of future development. Demand management, for example through water saving campaigns, has a role to play in making fuller use of existing infrastructure and reducing cumulative impacts of small scale development, where new infrastructure is harder to plan for or fund. This may be particularly important in those areas where increases in density are being sought.

10.11 Each water company now has a Water Resources Plan setting out how it proposes to maintain the supply/demand balance for the next 25 years. These plans are reviewed annually, rolled forward a year and scrutinised by the Environment Agency. In addition, the Environment Agency is developing a National and eight Regional Water Resources Strategies. In conjunction with Catchment Abstraction Management Strategies which the Agency will be providing on the basis of a 6 year cycle, these will provide a useful tool for the management of water resources, particularly in identifying the availability of water resources.

10.12 Furthermore, the Environment Agency is developing a national water quality strategy based on the aim of preventing deterioration and maintaining and improving water quality where possible. The European Bathing Water Directive and Urban Waste Water Directive are helping to improve the quality particularly of coastal waters. There is a substantial investment programme in order to comply with these directives.

Policy INF2

New development should be located and its implementation planned in such a way as to allow for sustainable provision of water services and enable timely investment in sewage treatment and discharge systems to maintain the appropriate standard of water quality. Techniques which improve water efficiency and minimise adverse impacts on water resources, on the quality, regime, and ecology of rivers, and on groundwater, should be encouraged. Redevelopment should identify and make provision for rectification of any legacy of contamination and drainage problems.

a   Development plans should:

   i   take water related issues into account from an early stage in the process of identifying land for development and redevelopment, to encourage the use of sites where past problems can be solved and seek to avoid sites where water supply and/or drainage provision is likely to be unsustainable;

   ii   co-ordinate the timing of new development with the provision of sustainable water supplies, sewage treatment and discharge systems in accordance with advice in PPG12 *(Development Plans)*; and

   iii   promote the introduction of water conservation measures and sustainable urban drainage solutions. Detailed supplementary planning guidance or site specific development briefs can help to facilitate the adoption of these measures.

b   In addition:

   i   local authorities should establish or maintain ongoing liaison with the Environment Agency, water companies and sewage statutory undertakers in order to ensure timely and sustainable provision of infrastructure for the supply of water and sewage treatment and discharge systems, particularly in connection with major new development; and

   ii   all relevant agencies and developers should encourage the incorporation of water conservation measures in new development, and promote public awareness of the need to reduce consumption.

Waste

10.13 The sustainable management of waste is an increasingly important issue facing modern society. It is a particularly critical issue for the South East which as a populous Region generates a large volume of waste and faces increasing difficulty in identifying new sites for waste disposal. The Government is concerned that provision is made for the re-use, recovery and disposal of waste, taking account of the potential for waste minimisation. The *Waste Strategy for England and Wales - Waste 2000* - published in May 2000, sets challenging targets to reduce the amount of industrial and commercial waste landfilled and to increase the recovery and recycling of municipal waste.

Box 6 - Principles of Waste Management

a   Best Practicable Environmental Option (BPEO)

This is a procedure which establishes for a given set of objectives, the option that provides the most benefits or the least damage to the environment as a whole, at acceptable cost, in the long term as well as the short term.

b   Regional Self-sufficiency

Most waste should be treated or disposed of within the region within which it is produced. Each region should provide for facilities with sufficient capacity to manage the quantity of waste expected to be needed to be dealt with in that area for at least 10 years. In some cases, however, it may be necessary to recognise units smaller than the region but larger than areas covered by Waste Planning Authorities.

c   Proximity Principle

Waste should generally be managed as near as possible to its place of production because transporting waste itself has an environmental impact.

d   Waste Hierarchy

This is a theoretical framework which should be considered when assessing the BPEO and it suggests that:

- The most effective environmental solution may often be to reduce the generation of waste i.e. reduction;
- Where further reduction is not practicable, products and materials can sometimes be used again, either for the same or for a different purpose i.e. re-use;
- Failing that, value should be recovered from waste, through recycling, composting or energy recovery from waste;
- If none of the above offer an appropriate solution waste should be disposed of.

Source: PPG10 (Planning and Waste Management)

10.14 The European Landfill Directive will be the key driver to reduce the amount of waste that requires final disposal to landfill. This will be achieved through additional recycling and other treatment technologies and waste minimisation. The Directive requires the amount of biodegradable municipal waste going to landfill to be reduced in three successive stages over a 15-20 year period. It will require substantial amount of municipal waste to be diverted away from landfill towards composting, recycling, energy from waste and other waste management technologies.

10.15 While waste generated within ROSE tends to be treated and disposed of within ROSE, most of the waste generated in London is transported for disposal to landfill sites in the rest of the Region. RPG3 *(Strategic Guidance for London Planning Authorities)* sets out current planning guidance for London based on the waste hierarchy and principles of sustainable development. This will be replaced by the Mayor of London's Spatial Development Strategy and Municipal Waste Management Strategy. It is unlikely that London will achieve self-sufficiency in the short term and disposal to landfill sites outside the capital will therefore continue to play an important role. However, the Mayor's strategies will be required to take account of Government policy and EU legislation and to make provision for the necessary waste management and disposal facilities to meet London's future needs for municipal and other waste streams so that there is a progressive reduction in the amount of untreated wastes exported to ROSE for disposal as alternative waste management facilities are established in London.

10.16   There is also scope for reducing the amount of inert material which is disposed of in landfill. Chapter 11 of this guidance points to the potential for recycling and re-using construction and demolition wastes, particularly in association with redevelopment in the South East. One of the resulting benefits may be a reduced demand for primary aggregates.

10.17   The use of rail and river transport for the movement of waste can considerably reduce the environmental impact that would otherwise be caused by lorry traffic. This is particularly true in London which can make use of the River Thames and an extensive rail network. In order to maintain and fully exploit these modes, however, the development of new waste transfer, management and disposal facilities along these routes is likely to be needed. Some parts of the Region also have access to rail and coastline but in other parts the opportunities for transferring to rail or water transport may be very limited. Chapter 9 of this guidance emphasises the need to safeguard rail freight facilities, wharves and port sites in the Region. Whilst transport by rail and river may be more desirable than by road, the most sustainable option is to manage waste as close as possible to the source. This can only occur if the planning system enables adequate provision to be made.

10.18   Close liaison will be needed with the Environment Agency to assess the current amount of waste generated in the Region, likely future trends and the need for waste management facilities. The Government wishes to see the development of the strategies for waste management at regional level by the Regional Technical Advisory Bodies (RTABs) as part of RPG. Further advice is set out in PPG10 (*Planning and Waste Management*) and in the national waste strategy, *Waste 2000*.

Policy INF3

Adequate provision should be made for the management of the Region's waste within its own boundaries wherever possible. Waste Planning Authorities should aim to make provision for a sufficient range and number of facilities for the re-use, recovery and disposal of waste that will need to be managed within their areas. Every effort should be made to minimise waste.

a   Until such time as targets for the management of waste at the regional level can be adopted, the following national targets should be used:

   i   to recycle or compost at least 25% of household waste by 2005, 30% by 2010 and 33% by 2015;

   ii   to recycle 17% of municipal waste by 2003 and at least 33% by 2015; and

   iii   by 2005, to reduce the amount of industrial and commercial waste going to landfill to 85% of 1998 levels.

b   Unitary development plans and waste local plans should:

   i   identify sites for waste treatment and disposal facilities having regard to the Best Practicable Environmental Option (BPEO), the waste hierarchy, the proximity

> principle and the regional self-sufficiency principle as advised in PPG10 *(Planning and Waste Management)*; and
>
> ii   integrate sites for waste treatment and disposal with rail and water-based transport systems wherever possible and where this is consistent with the proximity principle.
>
> c   In addition:
>
> i   local authorities should continue to collaborate with the waste industries and relevant agencies to actively promote waste minimisation and management processes such as re-use, recycling, incineration, energy recovery, composting and others in order to reduce the amount of waste produced and the amount of waste disposed of by landfill; and
>
> ii   a more integrated approach to waste management is required, with sufficient flexibility to enable full consideration of alternative and innovative waste management options. For example, recycling and composting schemes can provide an integrated, sustainable and cost effective means of managing waste locally.
>
> d   In reviewing this guidance, the Regional Planning Bodies and the Mayor of London will need to undertake further work to develop regional targets for waste management in the light of national waste management objectives and regional technical advice. They should also assess the need for regionally significant facilities for the management of waste.

Energy

10.19   During the past decade there has been an increasing shift away from carbon-intensive fuels such as coal and oil towards less carbon-intensive fuels such as gas and nuclear energy for many required energy supplies. With regard to energy used in transport there is still a reliance on carbon-intensive fuels. In view of the commitment to reducing carbon dioxide and other greenhouse gases, as expressed through international agreements on climate change, more energy will need to be supplied from energy sources which emit little or no carbon dioxide. The Government has set a target for 10% of UK electricity to be supplied from renewable sources by 2010, subject to the costs to consumers being acceptable. In support of this target the Government is developing a programme to ensure the further development of renewable energy sources and provide a framework for helping to achieve secure, economic and sustainable energy supplies, whilst protecting the environment.

10.20   The Region does contribute energy to the national grid, but on the whole the South East relies on energy supplies from other regions. It is likely that the Region will not be able to generate the full amount of energy which it needs in order to meet its own supply requirements. However, the Region's commitment to sustainable development will require greater recognition of the significant environmental, social and economic impacts arising both from energy generation and from current patterns of consumption, for example impacts arising from:

- resource exploitation;
- combustion of fossil fuels;
- transportation of fuel;
- local land use impacts of power generation facilities; and
- inefficient use of energy.

10.21   Renewable energy offers opportunities for increasing the diversity and security of energy supply, reducing harmful emissions to the environment, preserving finite fossil fuels for future generations, reducing the volume of waste to landfill through composting or energy from waste schemes and increasing opportunities for rural diversification, for example, by energy crops or deriving renewable energy from anaerobic digestion. The development and transport of renewable energy can, however, also have environmental disbenefits which need to be balanced against the wider benefits.

10.22 Annexes to PPG22 *(Renewable Energy)* identify a possible range of technologies which could have applications in the South East. They include energy from waste combustion, wood fuel, anaerobic digestion and landfill gas and active solar systems. Other technologies are also available including wind and tidal power. The Region's extensive areas of land which are designated for their environmental, landscape or cultural value, need to be protected and therefore, sensitivity is required in identifying suitable locations for renewable energy proposals. Chapter 6 provides further guidance on the protection of these areas and the need to develop within the wider countryside in ways which enhance the character of the area. Notwithstanding these constraints, various forms of renewable energy development, for example, those associated with the use of wood fuel, farming operations or energy crops, can be appropriate in rural areas. Studies on renewable energy provision are already being undertaken for the parts of the Region covered by the Government Offices for the South East and the East of England. The results will inform the Regional Sustainable Development Frameworks and also local planning activity.

10.23 Improved energy efficiency should be a key component of all types of development. The focus of this guidance on urban renaissance does offer scope for improving energy efficiency as part of urban renewal and redevelopment. An increasing demand for energy efficient design and appliances could also have economic and social advantages such as the development of new markets and products and cost savings for residents.

10.24 The demand for energy can be reduced, for example, by more effective insulation of buildings and through attention to energy efficiency best practice measures in design, layout and orientation of all building types, whether domestic or otherwise. Combined Heat and Power (CHP) as part of a local community heating scheme can increase energy savings to residents, as well as optimise reductions of carbon dioxide and contribute to urban renaissance. This highly fuel efficient technology provides substantial cost savings as well as environmental benefits. In new build or redevelopment schemes it needs to be considered at the earliest stage because of the infrastructure required. In respect of energy savings achieved through alternative transport infrastructure and reduced travel, further details are included in chapter 9 of this guidance.

Policy INF4

In planning the future development of the region and activities within it, priority should be given to energy conservation and to maximising the use of renewable energy sources as an alternative to fossil fuels.

a   Development plans should:

   i   include proposals for renewable energy resources, including active solar systems, wind power, energy from waste combustion, wood fuel, anaerobic digestion and landfill gas where these do not conflict with policies for the protection of designated areas contained in PPG7 *(The Countryside – Environmental Quality and Economic and Social Development)* and PPG9 *(Nature Conservation)*. Small scale schemes may be suitable in many parts of the rural areas;

   ii   promote energy efficient measures as part of the design and form of development; and

iii   encourage energy efficient technology such as CHP to form part of major new build or redevelopment proposals.

b   In addition:

    i   the Government's Environment and Energy Helpline and bodies such as the Energy Technology Support Unit (ETSU) can advise on how to increase energy efficiency and promote renewable energy sources. This may range from advice on CHP or community heating in industry or buildings to techniques for the life cycle assessment of buildings;

    ii   schemes such as the Energy Crops Scheme administered by the Ministry of Agriculture, Fisheries and Food or the use of woodland management strategies can contribute to increasing the potential for renewable energy as well as promoting economic activity; and

    iii   using their development control and building regulation processes, local authorities should seek to influence the design of new development to incorporate use of appropriate renewable energy heating or power systems.

c   The Regional Planning Bodies and the Mayor of London need to clarify how the Region will contribute to meeting the national target for the supply of electricity from renewable energy sources, taking account of regional studies of renewable energy provision.

Chapter 11

Minerals

11.1   Minerals are an important element in the economy of the South East, but their extraction can have a significant environmental impact. Government planning policies for minerals aim to ensure that there is an adequate supply, having regard to the objectives of sustainable development.

11.2   The South East has significant deposits of some minerals including sand and gravel for construction, clay, industrial sand and chalk. Rock, which can be crushed to make construction aggregate, occurs in parts of the South East but is generally of relatively low quality. The Region also has resources of fuller's earth, gypsum and hydrocarbons. Extraction of these materials will have land-use implications which will be subject to detailed local policies through development plans. There are also resources of marine sand and gravel in sea areas adjacent to the Region.

Production and Supply of Minerals

11.3   In 1997, the South East produced about 22 million tonnes of construction aggregates from the land and about 8 million tonnes of marine-dredged sand and gravel. In addition, some 4.1 million tonnes of chalk, 2 million tonnes of clay and 1.3 million tonnes of industrial sand are produced annually. Sand and gravel (from both land and sea) accounts for approximately 78% of the South East's mineral products, chalk 11% and clay 5%.

11.4   Supply patterns for most of the Region's minerals are essentially national. The exception, and quantitatively the most important, are construction aggregates. The Region's widespread reserves of sand and gravel have traditionally led to regional self-sufficiency. Most have been produced and consumed fairly near to centres of demand, mainly urban areas. Therefore environmentally unconstrained sites, where new extraction can take place, are becoming increasingly difficult to identify in many parts of the Region. This is especially the case in London which depends almost entirely on other areas for most of its supplies. London accounts for 20% of South East aggregates use. London does not have sufficient sand, gravel or crushed rock to meet its needs and currently imports 90% of its aggregates from other areas. The counties and London have agreed through the Regional Aggregates Working Party that London will meet the remaining 10% of its need for aggregates by extracting sand and gravel from land-won sources in London, based on an assessment of available and potential reserves in each area. London currently has sufficient identified resources to meet its 10% apportionment target for the period 1992-2006, based on current planning permissions for aggregates extraction and sites identified for potential aggregates extraction. Further sources, including increased use of recycled material, will need to be identified if London is to continue to meet this target beyond 2006.

11.5   Constraints on the availability of aggregates in the Region, and the lack of high quality hard rock, means that it has long been a significant importer of crushed rock, particularly from the South West and East Midlands. More recently, it has been receiving hard rock by sea from coastal quarries outside the Region, such as that at Glensanda in Scotland. The Region produced about 22 million tonnes of aggregates from the land in 1997, but consumed about 33 million tonnes of aggregates in the same year. Therefore about 33% of supply came from marine dredging and other areas. The Region is not self-sufficient in aggregates as recognised in Minerals Planning Guidance, MPG6 *(Guidelines for Aggregates Provision in England).*

11.6 In addition, alternative materials, including construction and demolition wastes, minerals wastes, some industrial wastes and by-products are also used as aggregates and meet part of the demand in the Region. The quantities used are not accurately known. However, the results of a survey of arising and use of construction and demolition waste is being published by the Environment Agency and other work is underway to secure information on the recycling of road planings.

Managing the Demand for Minerals

11.7 The Region is one of high demand for construction materials including sand, gravel and crushed rock from both within and outside the Region. However, it is also a source of alternative materials which are currently not fully used. The recycling of aggregates has local environmental impacts so suitable sites need to be chosen carefully. Modern forms of aggregate recycling could significantly reduce local impacts by such measures as containing the main crushing and sorting within an enclosed structure and the use of covered containers and water sprays to minimise dust. The Government has supported a trial Aggregates Advisory Service to disseminate information on, and increase awareness of, alternative materials and is considering how to secure a longer-term service.

11.8 Sustainable use of minerals can also be assisted by:

- avoiding the use of good quality primary aggregates wherever lower grade material would suffice;

- reducing waste in construction projects; and

- thinking carefully about where and how supplies might be secured for major development initiatives.

11.9 It is Government policy that more waste materials should be recycled, helping to reduce the need for primary extraction of aggregates, when that is the best practicable environmental option. The Government's strategy is set out in *Building A Better Quality Of Life: A Strategy For More Sustainable Construction* (DETR, 1999) and points out that the proportion of secondary and recycled aggregates used should be maximised to reduce the demand for primary aggregates and achieve greater local self-sufficiency in aggregates use. The strategy set out in this guidance for urban renaissance and for the reuse of previously-developed land is likely to generate opportunities for the recycling of building materials and consequently might reduce the demand for new aggregates.

11.10 Maximising the use of recycled materials can reduce the demand for primary aggregates, but it will still be necessary to import some aggregates from elsewhere and to identify sites within the Region where extraction is environmentally acceptable. MPG6 identified a need for 1,270 million tonnes of aggregates from within the South East over the period 1992-2006. It indicated that this should be met from a combination of locally land-won material, marine-dredged material, imports into the Region, and secondary and recycled aggregates. In terms of locally land-won material, MPG6 states that minerals planning authorities in the Region should make provision for 420 million tonnes of sand and gravel and 30 million tonnes of crushed rock over the period 1992-2006. It is thus accepted that the South East cannot be regionally self-sufficient.

11.11 Since 1994, it has become apparent that the estimates for national demand on which those figures were based were too high. MPG6 is to be reviewed shortly and will consider whether new targets should be set both for supply of primary aggregates and for higher levels of recycling of secondary and waste materials. The review is expected to be completed in 2001.

An early review of this chapter of RPG9 will be required and will need to be based on information provided by the Regional Aggregates Working Party for the South East, once a revised MPG6 is available.

Policy M1

Provision should be made for the supply of minerals, including both extraction and recycling of materials and aggregates. Wherever possible, the contribution made by substitute materials should be maximised. The regional contribution to the supply of aggregates shall be reassessed in an early review of this chapter of RPG9 following the publication of the revised MPG6.

a   Development plans should:

   i   conform with guidance in Minerals Planning Guidance Notes, MPG1 *(General Considerations and the Development Plan System)*, MPG6 *(Guidelines for Aggregates Provision in England)*, MPG10 *(Provision of Raw Material for the Cement Industry)* and MPG15 *(Provision of Silica Sand in England)*;

   ii   identify and safeguard mineral resources to ensure that there are sufficient environmentally acceptable sources to maintain an appropriate level of current and future supplies;

   iii   indicate in general terms areas within which sites for land-won mineral extraction should be safeguarded, taking account of guidance in PPG7 *(The Countryside and the Rural Economy)* and PPG9 *(Nature Conservation)*. For example, proposals, other than those of a minor nature, should not be located in the Areas of Outstanding Natural Beauty (AONBs) and the two proposed National Parks, except in exceptional circumstances and only after the most rigorous examination where they are demonstrated to be in the public interest. Similar considerations apply to proposed extractive operations which might affect other internationally or nationally designated areas including Special Protection Areas (SPAs) or Sites of Special Scientific Interest (SSSIs); and

   iv   identify and where necessary safeguard, sites suitable for facilities for the recycling, reprocessing and transfer of materials, for example for the recycling of construction and demolition materials, in accordance with guidance in PPG10 *(Planning and Waste Management)*.

b   In addition:

   i   local authorities should continue to encourage the minerals and construction industries in making efforts to maximise the proportion of secondary and recycled aggregates in order to reduce the demand in the Region for primary aggregates;

   ii   all those concerned with new development need to consider the resource implications and how construction materials will be secured at the least environmental cost, with greater public awareness of the need for materials and the implications in different parts of the Region;

   iii   major development and regeneration initiatives, such as in the Thames Gateway and PAERs, present significant opportunities for utilising alternative construction methods and substitute materials;

   iv   the implications of large-scale developments may be usefully discussed with the relevant mineral planning authorities and may include the development of additional recycling facilities; and

   v   where recycling facilities are required, their wider environmental benefits should be taken into account when considering local impacts.

Environmental Effects of Extraction and Recycling

11.12 Extraction of minerals can cause adverse environmental impacts such as noise, dust, effects of extraction on ground and surface water, and traffic. These effects can be mitigated by good management of sites. National guidance in MPG11 *(Controlling and Mitigating the Environmental Effects of Minerals Extraction in England)* is being revised and extended to deal with all environmental impacts. Extraction of minerals can also cause habitat destruction and land/soil degradation. However, land used for minerals extraction can be restored to appropriate beneficial uses which should, in general, conform with development plan policies for the area concerned. The implications of the European Landfill Directive and the targets which it has set for reducing the amount of biodegradable municipal waste going to landfill (see the section on waste in chapter 10) will imply a reducing role for waste disposal in minerals site restoration. Recycling operations can also cause adverse environmental impacts. A good practice guide is available on *Reducing the Environmental Effects of Recycled and Secondary Aggregates Production* (DETR, 2000).

11.13 A significant part of the disturbance caused by mineral working relates to associated traffic. It is Government policy that, where practicable, transport of minerals in bulk by rail or ship is preferable to long-distance road haulage. A significant part of the minerals imported into the Region comes already by rail and sea, but there may be opportunities to increase this. It is necessary to identify and, where appropriate, to safeguard suitable sites for rail depots and landing facilities at marine wharves and wharves on the River Thames for this purpose. The need for positive planning for rail and sea based freight is also considered in chapter 9 of this guidance.

Policy M2

The environmental impact of minerals extraction should be minimised through sound environmental management of extractive operations, high quality restoration and, where appropriate, aftercare of land affected by mineral extraction. The delivery of minerals by rail and ship should also be promoted.

a   Development plans should:

  i   include policies to ensure good management of sites both for mineral extraction and for recycling;

  ii   include policies and proposals for the restoration and aftercare of sites used for minerals extraction. This should be undertaken to high standards and further guidance is contained in MPG7 *(The Reclamation of Mineral Workings)*; and

  iii   identify and, where necessary, safeguard opportunities for the transportation of aggregates by rail and water.

b   In addition, partnership working will continue to be important between mineral planning authorities, the Environment Agency and the minerals industry in monitoring operations and the management and restoration of sites.

Chapter 12

Sub-Regional Areas

12.1 This guidance distinguishes between different parts of the Region, namely London, Thames Gateway, Priority Areas for Economic Regeneration (PAER), the Western Policy Area and Potential Growth Areas, as highlighted in the Core Strategy in chapter 4. While policies in chapters 5 to 11 apply throughout the Region, this chapter focuses on the different parts of the Region in more detail and emphasises the need for cross-boundary co-operation. For each sub-region this chapter highlights some of the issues or proposed studies which the relevant local authorities need to address jointly either through revisions to Regional Planning Guidance, or through individual development plans, local transport plans or other strategies, in partnership with key agencies and local communities.

Thames Gateway

12.2 This guidance identifies the Thames Gateway as a regional and national priority for regeneration and growth with the potential to make a major contribution to the Region's economy (see chapters 4 and 7). The area comprises a corridor of land extending from East London through North Kent and South Essex. It is unique in that it has its own sub-regional planning guidance - RPG9a – as well as being covered by RPG3b/9b. It lies within three Government Office Regions - London, the South East and East of England – and the Greater London Authority area and is covered by three Regional Development Agencies – SEEDA, EEDA and LDA. In addition, over 20 local authorities administer the sub-region. All these organisations together with a variety of strategic partnerships play an important part in taking forward the Thames Gateway initiative.

12.3 In view of the complexity of both the area itself and the issues involved, local authorities should co-operate closely with each other and with other stakeholders to ensure that there are consistent and coherent policies for the Thames Gateway, particularly in the production of development plans. The Government is considering proposals for creating new delivery mechanisms to bring forward key developments and has established a new Strategic Partnership with public, private and voluntary sector interests. This is supported by an Executive as a forum for the key public, private and voluntary sector interest. Co-ordination between the Regional Planning Bodies, the Mayor of London, Government Offices and Thames Gateway Executive will be necessary to determine the extent and timing of the review of RPG9a.

12.4 Socio-economic and physical problems within the Thames Gateway include high levels of deprivation, skills shortages, large areas of derelict land, weak transport infrastructure and environmental degradation. However, a major advantage of this area is its proximity to Central London, continental Europe and major transport hubs. Its location and the availability of large sites, extensive areas of land with potential for redevelopment and access to a surplus labour supply, means that this sub-region is capable of accommodating substantial sustainable growth. General environmental improvement and major development and transport projects such as the Channel Tunnel Rail Link, the Ebbsfleet Valley and Stratford International Railway Stations, Bluewater and the Millennium Dome, are already acting as catalysts for improving the area's image thereby attracting further inward investment.

12.5 The scale of the further development potential in the Thames Gateway area makes it unique in the Region. It also presents a vital opportunity for creating more sustainable forms of development in the future. In order to maximise this opportunity development should occur in a planned way within the framework of RPG9a.

12.6 Long term commitment to the Thames Gateway has already been demonstrated by central and local Government, and the private and public sector partnerships. The Regional Development Agencies in particular will have an important co-ordinating role in future initiatives for the assembly and redevelopment of land. The strategies drawn up by the Regional Development Agencies and the Greater London Authority will be vital in identifying and bringing forward an adequate supply of land to meet regeneration needs.

12.7 The implementation of transport schemes such as the A13 realignment and the Jubilee line extension have been particularly successful in the Thames Gateway in improving accessibility and relieving congestion. However, further strategic transport proposals, to be identified in Local Transport Plans, will be essential as they will be of major importance in establishing a sustainable framework upon which to locate new development. A significant amount of regeneration funding has already been injected into Thames Gateway projects so far, which aim to support and strengthen the community. There is a need to build on this and also for partnership between local authorities, schools, higher/further educational establishments and the Learning Skills Councils to increase the local skills and educational standards of existing and future communities. Equally important is the establishment of balanced communities with appropriate and accessible community infrastructure such as schools, colleges, hospitals and enhanced cultural facilities.

12.8 **Joint working is required to:**

a   develop mechanisms to deliver the long term vision set out in RPG9a through the new Strategic Partnership, including enhanced co-ordination and targeting of public and private investment.

b   increase the local skills and educational standards of existing and future communities through partnerships between local authorities, schools, higher/further educational establishments and the Learning Skills Councils.

c   ensure that regeneration is achieved in line with sustainable development principles:

   i   development should focus on schemes which:

   • recycle previously used land close to potential sustainable transport networks;

   • provide high quality environments with good design and a mix of land uses;

   • protect special features such as the River Thames and nationally and internationally designated wildlife sites; and

   • enable balanced communities with appropriate and accessible community infrastructure such as schools, colleges, hospitals and enhanced cultural facilities.

   ii   local planning authorities need to produce clear development strategies for their areas which promote sustainable patterns of development by allocating areas and locations for major growth in accordance with advice, for example, in PPG3 *(Housing)* and PPG6 *(Town Centres and Retail Developments)* and to help achieve the longer term vision set out in RPG9a.

d   agree the extent of an early review of RPG9a, to be initiated by the Regional Planning Bodies and Mayor of London in consultation with the Government Offices.

Priority Areas for Economic Regeneration (PAERs)

12.9   All the areas identified as PAERs need tailored regeneration strategies backed up by appropriate resources to address their problems and maximise their contribution to the sustainable development of the region. Designation as PAER signals to regional partners, including the Regional Development Agencies, that the needs of the area should be given high priority.

South Hampshire, Southampton and Portsmouth

12.10   This sub-region consists of the administrative districts of Southampton, Eastleigh, Fareham, Gosport, Portsmouth and Havant and parts of New Forest, Test Valley and Winchester. It contains the two cities of Southampton and Portsmouth which are the two largest cities in the South East outside London. Portsmouth and Southampton are major centres of employment which exert a powerful influence within the local and regional economy. The area also provides important social and cultural services for the region. The area has two major seaports, particularly Southampton which is the Region's largest international deep sea port. In addition, the area includes Southampton International Airport and has established links with London and the rest of the United Kingdom and Europe. The urban areas in the sub-region are surrounded by undeveloped coast and countryside, including the New Forest Heritage Area (the Countryside Agency has begun the process of designating the New Forest as a National Park.)

12.11   Although the area enjoys general prosperity, there is a pronounced incidence of local deprivation, which is exacerbated by a skills mismatch between the requirements of jobs created by new industries and the relatively unskilled nature of a relatively high proportion of the resident workforce. Skills enhancement will be an important element of a strategy to enable the unemployed and under employed to access those jobs that already exist in the sub-region and those that could be attracted to it in the future. Locational mismatch has developed with the main areas of lower cost and affordable housing being primarily in the older urban areas of Gosport, Portsmouth and Southampton and some of their peripheral estates while the growing employment focal points include decentralised locations along the M27. More affordable housing is needed in the more prosperous suburban areas where a need is being created and not met, and from where it is also easier to access the new employment areas.

12.12   At the same time, the area has significant potential for economic growth. The attractiveness of the area for business includes strong local universities, existing clusters of high tech industry, rail and motorway access, international ports and airport, good quality development sites and an increasing emphasis on cultural facilities. As the largest urban area in the Region outside London, the sub-region has sizeable needs and opportunities for urban renewal including additional housing.

12.13   **Joint working is required to:**

a   develop complementary strategies through development plans, local transport plans and other local strategies which particularly:

i   maximise the area's economic potential while ensuring that all sectors of society are included in the economy and making best use of the available land and communications infrastructure;

ii   maximise the potential for urban renaissance and mixed communities also in suburban parts of the urban areas, including better use of land and provision of affordable housing in locations easily accessible to new employment areas; and

iii   enable social inclusion.

b   target funding and assistance to tackle deprivation and enhance skills.

c   ensure genuine multi-modal access in a north and south direction to the port to allow it to better serve inland markets beyond the South East. Any proposal for expansion of the Port of Southampton will need to take account of the wider spatial strategy and its environmental, social and economic objectives.

The Isle of Wight

12.14   The Isle of Wight is both a PAER and a Rural Priority Area. It is administered by the Isle of Wight Council. A substantial area of the Island is designated as Areas of Outstanding Natural Beauty (AONB), while much of its coastline is designated Heritage Coast. Areas of land and stretches of coastline are also designated for their international and national importance for wildlife.

12.15   The island has a long history as a holiday location and there is a need to encourage appropriate tourist facilities, while protecting the local environment. In diversifying the rural economy of the island, local partners will need to ensure that all sectors of the local community are involved in the economy and that it is sensitive to the natural resources and landscape and cultural features. As an island economy it has particular characteristics and needs. Tailored solutions will be required to tackle the problems of unemployment and deprivation experienced on the island. The development of local supply chains will be important as will facilitating the growth of business clusters which do not depend on the transport of large amounts of goods. Skills enhancement will be an important part of the strategy to tackle deprivation and social exclusion. Furthermore, communication between the island and the mainland are vital to the island's economy.

12.16   **Joint working is required to:**

a   develop tailored regeneration strategies which particularly:

i   enhance skills;

ii   develop local supply chains and enterprises not dependent on the transport of large amounts of goods; and

iii   enable appropriate tourist facilities while protecting the environment.

b   improve communications between the island and the mainland as part of a sustainable transport strategy through the development plans, local transport plans and partnership working with transport operators.

Sussex Coast and Towns

12.17   The area identified as a PAER extends along the Sussex coast from Shoreham Harbour in the west to Hastings in the east, and lies within the counties of East and West Sussex and the unitary authority of Brighton & Hove. It includes the major built-up areas of Hove, Brighton, Eastbourne and Hastings, as well as other towns such as Shoreham and Bexhill. Its infrastructure includes the commercial ports of Newhaven (which has a ferry link to Dieppe) and Shoreham (which also has a small airport).

12.18   The urban areas are concentrated along the coastal zone and surrounded by the Sussex Downs Area of Outstanding Natural Beauty (AONB) which the Countryside Agency is considering for designation as part of the proposed South Downs National Park. In addition, there are a number of sites designated as Special Areas of Conservation and National Nature Reserves, the High Weald AONB near Hastings and Bexhill and part of the coastline west of Eastbourne is designated Heritage Coast.

12.19 The larger coastal towns contain significant pockets of deprivation and unemployment associated with the decline of the traditional tourist industry as well as the mismatch between the pool of labour and available jobs. In addition to higher levels of unemployment, the coastal towns are also characterised by poor quality older housing, low educational attainment, high youth unemployment and rising juvenile crime. Funding programmes have targeted areas in greatest need, particularly in Brighton and Hove and Hastings. For example, Hastings has been designated as an Objective 2 Area under European Regional Policy and is therefore eligible for European Structural Funds.

12.20 There are good communications between London, Gatwick and Brighton and Hove by means of the M23/A23 and A24, and rapid rail services. There are also coastal inter-urban road and rail routes although these are poorer, especially in the eastern part of the sub-region. Improvements to the transport networks, particularly the coastal rail links, could also enhance the advantages of the area's proximity to northern France. Transport studies are currently taking place to consider particularly the east-west communication links, examining Access to Hastings and the A27 Worthing to Lancing, and Southampton to Folkestone routes (refer to chapter 9). In addition, the Thameslink 2000 project and ports study will also play a part in addressing issues of remoteness, facilitating the development of employment sites and improving access to the ports.

12.21 There is potential for business and industrial employment-generating uses to build upon the area's arts, culture and media industries as well as its education and training facilities, particularly in Brighton and Hove. The attractive countryside and coastal location also provide opportunities for developing further sustainable tourism related activities.

12.22 **Joint working is required to:**

a progress proposals emerging from the multi-modal studies, the Thameslink 2000 project and the wider ports study (referred to in chapter 9) through the review of this guidance and through local transport plans as appropriate.

b explore the process by which Brighton and other coastal towns may benefit from economic growth in the Crawley/Gatwick Area through a joint study to inform development plans and other strategies.

c develop complementary strategies through development plans, local transport plans and other strategies which, in particular:

  i maximise the economic potential of tourism, arts, cultural and media activities;

  ii enable the regeneration of the ports, including access to them;

  iii ensure protection and enhancement of the Areas of Outstanding Natural Beauty; and

  iv manage flood risk and protect the coastal zone.

d target funding and assistance to tackle deprivation and enhance skills.

East Kent

12.23 The area includes an arc of nine coastal towns in east Kent in the local authority areas of Canterbury, Thanet, Dover and Shepway. The coastal towns extend from Whitstable in the north, through Herne Bay, Margate, Broadstairs, Ramsgate, Deal, Dover and Folkestone to Hythe in the south and are categorised as Priority Areas for Economic Regeneration. Part of Thanet, with one of the highest levels of unemployment in the UK and the Sandwich ward of Dover are designated Objective 2 areas (under European Regional Policy). The coastal area has experienced the cumulative effects of decline in a number of traditional industries. In particular, the problems of the area include a declining ferry port industry as a consequence of the channel tunnel, the aftermath of the closure of the East Kent coal-field, the loss of the holiday trade and the perception of remoteness.

12.24 The sub-region also includes two former coal-fields. These comprise a larger area within the Dover administrative area which stretches from Aylesham in the west to the outer suburbs of Deal to the east, and includes Eastry to the north and Lower Eythorne and East Studal to the south, and a much smaller area to the north west within Canterbury district centred on Hersden. The former coal-field area includes the four former colliery sites and buildings at Snowdown, Tilmanstone, Betteshanger and Chislet (Hersden). The dependence upon one key sector and the lack of new investment in the area has created a range of social, economic and environmental problems. In contrast to the image of the county as a prosperous and picturesque region, the Kent coal-fields have been left with a legacy of derelict land, redundant and dilapidated buildings, low educational and skills levels and long term male unemployment of over 50%. To help overcome these problems the Kent coal-fields are also designated as a Rural Priority Area.

12.25 The development of infrastructure and port diversification is seen as the springboard for economic regeneration. Despite the constraint imposed by good quality agricultural land surrounding the towns (especially Thanet), a large amount of industrial and business land is available. It is clear therefore that generally the provision of new employment land in the coastal area is less important than other factors in attracting investment. The quality of infrastructure and the availability of trained labour are two important factors, but of equal importance are those aspects which contribute to the quality of life; attributes such as the quality and type of available housing, the quality of the environment, range and quality of shopping and leisure facilities in towns, and the quality of schools in the area.

12.26 Opportunities arise for further development initiatives such as those which have resulted from the growth of the pharmaceutical research and development at Richborough, business park investment at Manston, the Ramsgate harbour tunnel link and the growth in container and cruise traffic at Dover. The area also benefits from its attractive coastal location and an outstanding range of historic monuments and buildings. Furthermore, the completion of the Channel Tunnel Rail Link (see chapter 9) will in future enhance the area's locational advantage by improving access with the rest of Europe.

12.27 **Joint working is required to develop and implement complementary strategies through development plans, local transport plans and other local strategies, which:**

    a   maximise the current and future locational advantages of the area;

    b   encourage capital investment through environmental improvements and improved infrastructure, particularly for communications; and

    c   assist people entering or re-entering the job market.

Harlow

12.28 Harlow was one of the earliest of the post-war New Towns. Harlow District has tightly constrained boundaries and lies between Epping Forest District in Essex and East Hertfordshire District in the county of Hertfordshire.

12.29 In recent years, Harlow town has faced continuing manufacturing decline and social deprivation. Its building stock is becoming progressively more obsolete, and the town centre is in need of regeneration and renewal. The 1998 Index of Local Deprivation records Harlow as the most deprived former New Town district in the South East. Economic restructuring is taking place, but substantial levels of investment are needed if Harlow is to fulfil its potential.

12.30 The town has numerous locational strengths. It lies close to London Stansted Airport, and is roughly mid-way between the emerging centre of London Docklands and the buoyant high-technology-based Cambridge economy. Harlow is also host to several major companies, and has a relatively youthful labour force. However, physical expansion of the built-up area could be constrained by the Metropolitan Green Belt.

12.31 **Joint working is required to:**

   a   consider the needs and potential of Harlow – in particular the scope to draw benefit from its proximity to London Stansted Airport – as part of the London-Stansted-Cambridge sub-regional study to be taken forward in line with other policies in this guidance; and

   b   develop complementary strategies in development plans, local transport plans and other strategies to encourage capital investment in Harlow through environmental improvements, improved infrastructure, and provision for increased learning and skills training.

East London/Lower Lea Valley

12.32   This guidance identifies a PAER in East London and the Lower Lea Valley, extending from London Docklands up to and including the urban areas of Waltham Cross, Cheshunt, and Hoddesdon in Hertfordshire. A number of local planning authorities, both in London and the East of England, cover this area.

12.33   The area has some of the worst concentrations of urban deprivation and unemployment in the country in terms of both extent and intensity. Overall, the need for urban renaissance is as pressing here as anywhere in the country. However, the area has significant assets. These include the recently-opened Jubilee Line extension and the developing major public transport interchange at Stratford which is to be further enhanced by an international station on the Channel Tunnel Rail Link. The Lee Valley Regional Park and Epping Forest provide strategic environmental and leisure attractions. The area adjoins the growing commercial centre of Canary Wharf in London Docklands, and is well-located with respect to London Stansted Airport and the buoyant economy of Cambridge. There is also a large labour force and tracts of vacant previously-used land which represent a significant development opportunity, particularly to build upon the existing large concentration of manufacturing industries. However, existing urban areas are tightly constrained by the Metropolitan Green Belt.

12.34 **Joint working is required to:**

   a   consider the needs and potential of the East London/Lower Lea Valley area as part of the London-Stansted-Cambridge sub-regional study to be taken forward in line with other policies in this guidance; and

   b   develop complementary strategies to improve social, economic, environmental and transport conditions in the area.

Luton/Dunstable/Houghton Regis

12.35   The area comprises three linked towns, Luton, Dunstable and Houghton Regis within the districts of Luton and South Bedfordshire. Bedfordshire County Council and Luton Unitary Authority are joint structure plan authorities for the wider area.

12.36   The area has an advantageous location situated between London and Milton Keynes. North-south rail communications, including frequent services to London and the East Midlands, are good. Implementation of the Thameslink 2000 proposals will further enhance rail links to London and the wider South East. However, strategic road routes, especially the M1, are under pressure. Options for the future transportation strategy are being considered in the London-South Midlands multi-modal study. East–west communications are poor and would benefit from enhancement. There is also severe congestion on the local road network. The proposed Translink guided busway is an illustration of the infrastructure investment that may be needed to address this.

12.37 London Luton Airport, with its planned growth to ten million passengers per annum and the associated Luton Airport Parkway rail station, has the potential to act as a catalyst for major employment growth and wealth-generation in the area. It will be important to realise this potential in a way that benefits all sections of the community, and which does not harm the local environment. The longer term future of the airport is being considered as part of the study of airports in the South East and East of England (see chapter 9).

12.38 Although the area still relies heavily on its manufacturing base (dominated by motor vehicle production), this has narrowed considerably following major closures and contractions. This has resulted in pockets of high unemployment. Major economic restructuring and regeneration is already taking place in the area, but more is needed to diversify the employment base and alleviate localised social stresses and skills mismatches. The distinctive and diverse needs of the large ethnic community must also be recognised. Many wards have been designated as an Assisted Area (Tier 2 and Tier 3) and/or an Objective 2 Area, as a means to accelerate the process of regeneration alongside existing regeneration initiatives such as the Luton Dunstable Partnership.

12.39 There are reserves of previously-used land and buildings in the urban area which provide an opportunity for redevelopment, but much of this requires considerable remedial treatment. Some of these sites are allocated for employment use, although these allocations may need to be reviewed to take account of the advice elsewhere in this guidance and in PPG3 *(Housing)*, and the potential wider benefits of other uses and mixed use developments. Recent developments, including Luton University, have assisted the process of urban regeneration and need to be sustained in order to create a secure foundation for urban renaissance.

12.40 The towns are among the most densely populated outside Greater London and are tightly constrained by the South Bedfordshire Green Belt. They are also in close proximity to the Chilterns Area of Outstanding Natural Beauty and the Luton Hoo Estate. Overall, the area represents a significant opportunity for attracting major new inward investment, but the level of investment needed may be high if the area is to fulfil its full potential.

12.41 **Joint working is required to:**

a   progress proposals emerging from the multi-modal studies through the review of this guidance and through local transport plans as appropriate;

b   develop complementary strategies through development plans and other strategies which, in particular:

   i   review the allocations of employment land and encourage development proposals and land uses that contribute to economic restructuring and sustainable urban regeneration; and

   ii   realise the potential of London Luton Airport in accordance with sustainability objectives.

Tendring Coast

12.42 The area comprises the port of Harwich and the seaside resorts of Clacton and Walton. Tendring District Council is the Local Planning Authority, and Essex County Council the Structure Plan authority.

12.43 Major economic restructuring is taking place on the Tendring coast and substantial levels of investment may be needed for it to fulfil its potential. Harwich has been hit by redundancies in its port operations, while Clacton and Walton have been affected by changes in the tourism industry on which they have traditionally depended. The three towns have high unemployment rates and poor job prospects. Their relative remoteness and poor accessibility has hindered efforts to provide alternative employment, but their need for economic diversification remains. Most wards have Assisted Area (Tier 3) status, which could be exploited both to strengthen the towns' current roles and to diversify into other activities. There is also a small Rural Priority Area just inland of the towns.

12.44 Harwich requires investment in its port infrastructure and its links to other areas, if its role is to grow and prosper. The multi-modal study of the London-Ipswich corridor, programmed to start in 2000-2001, should provide a base for determining the necessary improvements to the links to Harwich. Clacton, Harwich and Walton are all relatively small towns in need of urban regeneration and a diversified economy. The aim is to promote a form of 'urban renaissance' in the towns appropriate to their size, location and character. It is essential that the area's regeneration goals are met without detriment to the important coastal and estuarine habitats.

12.45 **Joint working is required to:**

a   progress proposals emerging from the multi-modal studies and the wider ports study (referred to in chapter 9) through the review of this guidance and through local transport plans as appropriate; and

b   develop complementary strategies through development plans and other strategies which, in particular:

   i   enable the area to benefit from emerging tourism markets and other economic activities; and

   ii   enhance the coastal and estuarine habitats.

Western Policy Area

12.46 The Western Policy Area, as explained in the Core Strategy (see chapter 4), is a notional description of the area to the west and south of London. In order to achieve sustainable development, further growth in this part of the Region needs to occur in a form which minimises the additional pressures on land and labour resources, particularly in 'hotspots' where positive action is required. Further guidance is provided in chapter 7.

12.47 Throughout the Western Policy Area local authorities need to collaborate in tackling the problems in particular hotspots. However, this chapter highlights three particular sub-regions within the Western Policy Area where local authorities can build upon the collaborative approaches which they have already initiated, in order to tackle cross-boundary issues.

Thames Valley

12.48 For the purpose of this guidance, the Thames Valley sub-region covers the area of the Berkshire Unitary Authorities, South Oxfordshire, Oxford, Chiltern, South Buckinghamshire, Wycombe, Basingstoke and Dean districts and parts of West London.

12.49 In common with other parts of the Western Policy Area, this sub-region is characterised by concentrations of business service employment and high tech, knowledge-based industries and by the increasing pressure on local infrastructure, land resources and house prices. This sub-region is one of the most prosperous areas in the UK and the proximity of London and Heathrow Airport encourages businesses to locate here. Although transport systems are generally good, there are considerable pressures on the transport network and a need for improved public transport links to Heathrow, which are reflected in the number of proposals and transport studies targeting the area (see chapter 9).

12.50 **Joint working is required to:**

a   progress proposals emerging from the multi-modal studies (referred to in chapter 9) through the review of this guidance and through local transport plans as appropriate;

b   develop complementary strategies through development plans, local transport plans and other strategies which, in particular:

    i   improve public transport links to Heathrow; and

    ii   enable existing and emerging business clusters to develop in a sustainable way.

The Blackwater Valley

12.51   The Blackwater Valley encompasses all or parts of the administrative districts of Surrey Heath, Waverley and Guildford in Surrey; Bracknell Forest and Wokingham in Berkshire; and Hart and Rushmoor in Hampshire. The Valley runs in a south to north-west direction and covers the larger towns of Farnham, Aldershot, Farnborough and Camberley, and several smaller settlements including Ash, Frimley Green, Blackwater and Sandhurst. Although in proximity to each other, these are clearly distinguishable as separate settlements.

12.52   The area is connected north-south by the A331 (Blackwater Valley Road) and A325, and east-west by the M3, A30 and A31. The railway network also links the larger towns. The area enjoys reasonable proximity to both Heathrow and Gatwick airports. Whilst the initial impression is that the area is quite well served by the transport system, closer analysis reveals that there are shortcomings in the rail network, particularly the poor relationship between north-south and east-west links. Evidence also indicates that there is no significant capacity in the rail network to serve additional commuters, with the likely consequence that any new development would increase levels of car-borne commuting. There is therefore a need for improvements to the public transport systems.

12.53   The towns in the Blackwater Valley experienced significant expansion in the 1960s and 1970s and generally enjoy a buoyant economy. There is now pressure for further residential and employment development yet the area is partly constrained by the Green Belt and environmental designations of international importance. Through the Blackwater Valley network of local authorities, efforts are being made to avoid problems of fragmentary initiatives in this area. If future economic growth is to take place, further collaboration will be required to ensure a co-ordinated approach to land-use and transport planning, making best use of the existing urban areas and infrastructure.

12.54   **Joint working will be required to:**

a   undertake a study to assist in optimising the future economic growth in the area. Such a study could clarify the extent of the Blackwater Valley sub-region and identify the best locations for economic growth on the basis of taking advantage of local potential. It should help to identify areas where labour supply is constraining growth and take positive measures to relieve this problem, either by the provision of more housing or by the improvement of public transport; and

b   reflect any agreed strategy for the area in development plans, local transport plans and other relevant strategies.

The Crawley/Gatwick/M23 Area

12.55   This sub-regional area is centred on Crawley, Gatwick and Horley, but its influence extends to Horsham, East Grinstead, Redhill and Reigate, Haywards Heath, the South Coast and, to a lesser extent, south London. It is traversed north/south by the M23/A23, connecting London to Brighton, which also enjoy fast rail links.

12.56 Gatwick Airport is the single most important element of the area's economy, and is of significant economic importance to the Region as a whole. The longer term future of Gatwick Airport is being examined in the study of airports in the South East and East of England (see chapter 9). However, within the period of this guidance, British Airports Authority hopes to expand the passenger throughput at Gatwick Airport from the current 30 million passengers per year to 40 million by 2008. This would be within the constraints of the existing single runway and two terminals. The airport has helped to foster clusters of employment in the chemical and pharmaceutical industries, and financial services. There are also a number of aviation-related industries in Crawley.

12.57 This anticipated growth at Gatwick Airport may be expected to generate further demand for labour within the area. For example, some forecasts suggest that the number of airport-related jobs may increase by about 11,000. Demand for labour will need to be met if the economic benefits associated with the airport are to be maximised. However, there is currently little surplus labour to draw upon locally.

12.58 **Joint working is required to:**

a   explore the process by which Brighton and other coastal towns may benefit from economic growth in the Crawley/Gatwick Area through a study to inform development plans and other strategies; and

b   develop complementary strategies through development plans, local transport plans and other strategies, to meet the demand for labour. In particular:

   •   providing housing in accessible locations locally and enabling the provision of associated infrastructure including health, education and other community facilities; and

   •   enabling improved access to Gatwick Airport (see chapter 9).

Potential Growth Areas

12.59 Studies are proposed to examine the need and scope for additional growth in the following three areas.

Milton Keynes

12.60 This sub-region is not defined by administrative boundaries; it includes Milton Keynes Unitary Authority and large parts of Buckinghamshire, Bedfordshire and Northamptonshire.

12.61 Milton Keynes has been very successful in achieving economic and housing growth over the last 30 years, and has been the fastest growing area in the UK in that time. It remains one of the powerhouses of the Region; currently planned rates of growth should continue with any necessary adjustments made in the light of an interregional study. Future growth will need to focus on high quality design and on achieving a sustainable pattern of development of mixed and balanced communities. It will not be intended to meet all the Region's needs, but to enable the success of the city to continue into the future without compromising the attractiveness of the area.

12.62 **An interregional study should be undertaken to consider the further development potential of the Milton Keynes sub-region.**

a   The study should:

   i   define the extent of the Milton Keynes sub-region;

    ii   establish a clear vision of the long-term potential household and employment growth in the area, assuming that Milton Keynes will continue to expand and perform a major role in accommodating and stimulating regional growth over the next 20-30 years;

    iii   identify options for achieving a sustainable pattern of development, including more intensive use of land, the sequential approach, and the use of high quality design;

    iv   propose the broad distribution of dwellings in the sub-region concomitant with Milton Keynes' growth needs;

    v   incorporate proposals and mechanisms for planning and implementing growth across local authority and regional boundaries; and

    vi   identify the mechanisms for implementation and the provision of infrastructure.

  b   The study should be led jointly by the respective regional planning bodies and involving the local authorities in the area, the appropriate Government Offices, the Regional Development Agencies, English Partnerships, business and other key interested partners.

  c   The study should aim to be completed within a year of commencement. The study, and its examination through individual structure plan processes, will inform the next reviews of RPGs for the South East, East of England and East Midlands.

Ashford

12.63 The town of Ashford, with a population of 50,000, is situated 50 miles from London in the heartland of Kent. For many years the town has been identified in the Kent Structure Plan as a growth point, with substantial housing development (700 dwellings per year over a 20-year period) alongside economic development. Plan implementation has been slow because of reluctance in the market to exploit the real potential of the area, although there has been an increase in pace with the completion of the M20 and more recently the international railway station. Well located as a nodal point for sub-regional, national and international communications, Ashford will benefit in due course from the completion of the Channel Tunnel Rail Link. It is proposed that links between East Kent, Ashford and Channel Tunnel be investigated as part of an expanded multi-modal study see chapter 9).

12.64 The town is relatively unconstrained by high quality agricultural land or other landscape designations on its southern side and there is significant potential for developing the town to take advantage of its manifest locational advantages and all that has already been achieved. At the same time, growth needs to occur in a way which is more energy efficient, makes more sustainable use of natural resources, especially water, minimises the risk of flooding and does not increase the pollution of air, land and water.

12.65 **The local authorities should initiate an early study in association with the Regional Planning Body, the South East of England Development Agency and the Government Office to assess the scope for growth at Ashford and how to achieve it.**

London-Stansted-Cambridge Sub-Region

12.66 This guidance acknowledges that the London-Stansted-Cambridge sub-region may have the potential to accommodate major sustainable growth. The sub-region extends from London Docklands to Cambridge in East Anglia. At its southern end, it includes London Boroughs with some of the most severe social and economic deprivation in England but with major regeneration potential which will be enhanced by the development of Stratford International station on the CTRL. These are within the East London/Lower Lea Valley PAER, described previously. At the northern end, Cambridge is one of the most buoyant local economies in the country, with particular strengths in the high technology, biotechnology and R&D sectors. Between these lies the Harlow PAER and London Stansted Airport.

12.67 London Stansted Airport has a planned growth to 15 million passengers per annum. It is a major freight mover, being the third busiest airport for freight after Heathrow and Gatwick. Its longer term future is being examined in the study of airports in the South East and East of England (see chapter 9). It has good north-south transport links by both road and rail, with fast links to London and direct services to Cambridge, the midlands and north. East-west communications are less well-developed, but improvements to the A120 are programmed. Housing allocations to support employment growth at the airport have been made in both the Essex and Hertfordshire Structure Plans. These have been predominantly in Bishop's Stortford, Braintree, Harlow and some of the smaller towns in Uttlesford District (Essex). There are extensive areas of Metropolitan Green Belt to the south of the airport, and areas of the best and most versatile agricultural land to the north.

12.68 **An interregional study should be undertaken to investigate what the nature, possible extent and location of future growth might be within the London-Stansted-Cambridge area.**

a   The study should cover parts of Greater London, Essex, Hertfordshire and Cambridgeshire and will need to be advised by the study of development options in the Cambridge Sub-Region proposed in the *Regional Planning Guidance for East Anglia* (RPG6).

b   The study should:

i   look at economic potential and development pressures in the sub-region;

ii   examine a range of options (including continuance of existing policies) to address identified development needs, taking account of the scale, location, timing, economic consequences, environmental impacts, infrastructure needs and implementation mechanisms of any proposed level of growth. It should draw on emerging Government airports policy; and

iii   explicitly consider the potential effects of economic growth and development needs in the London-Stansted-Cambridge sub-region on the East London/Lower Lea Valley and Harlow PAERs – particularly whether such growth would assist or inhibit regeneration in those areas – and also the possible impacts on areas outside the sub-region, such as the Thames Gateway.

c   The study should be undertaken by a range of agencies including the Mayor of London, the Regional Planning Body for the East of England, and the strategic planning authorities and RDAs in the study area.

d   The sub-regional study should inform the production of a sub-regional strategy. This in turn would need to be jointly agreed by the Mayor of London and the Regional Planning Body for the East of England to inform the London Spatial Development Strategy and RPG for the East of England. It would also provide a context for the review of development plans and RDA strategies.

Chapter 13

Implementation, Monitoring and Review

Implementation

13.1 The role of RPG9 is to provide spatial guidance to achieve regional objectives. The policies set out in this guidance provide a framework for development plans, local transport plans, a longer term planning framework for the strategies of the Regional Development Agencies – SEEDA, EEDA and the LDA – as well as informing other strategies and programmes throughout the Region.

13.2 Reference is made throughout this guidance to the range of planning and other mechanisms available to implement the guidance. Local authorities and Regional Development Agencies, require the co-operation of a large number of agencies and bodies in the private, public and voluntary sectors if they are to be successful in implementing this guidance. Public investment will continue to be required to improve infrastructure and urban management schemes and public-private partnerships and developer contributions should assist in the delivery of the strategy set out in this guidance.

13.3 In preparing their development plans local authorities need to be as inclusive as possible, involving all sectors of the local community, including the business community. It will be important to consult with education and health authorities and health trusts, to ensure that the education and health implications of draft strategies are properly examined. Innovative approaches can help increase participation in the process. Local Agenda 21 strategies and community strategies can play an important part in stimulating local involvement in the preparation of other local strategies. However local authorities should not lose sight of the need to have up-to-date development plans in place and to ensure that revisions or replacements are prepared speedily in accordance with the advice in PPG 12 *(Development Plans)*.

Inter- and Intra-Regional Co-ordination

13.4 Implementation of this guidance will also require close co-operation with neighbouring regions. In particular, the preparation of revised Regional Planning Guidance for the *East of England* (RPG6), *South West* (RPG10), *East Midlands* (RPG8) and *West Midlands* (RPG11), should consider the cross-boundary issues and relevant content of this Guidance. The new Regional Planning Bodies and the Mayor of London will need to ensure that the arrangements for co-ordinating future work are effective.

13.5 Within the Region, local authorities may also need to co-operate in preparing and implementing sub-regional strategies as advised in chapter 12. There are various mechanisms by which local authorities and regions can co-operate with their neighbours on sub-regional strategies. They include:

- formal and informal partnerships;

- joint development plans;

- joint studies to inform the preparation of adjoining development plans;

- joint local transport plans or joint studies to inform the preparation of adjoining local transport plans;

- strategies covering more than one local authority, for example, for coastal or countryside management plans;

- transnational spatial planning projects, for example, under the European Union funded Interreg Programme.

Monitoring

13.6   Monitoring of this RPG needs to be carried out on a regular basis to assess whether the policies are being sufficiently implemented and having their desired effect. It is important that monitoring is not merely a matter of general intelligence gathering, but involves the analysis of actual data relevant to the regional circumstances of the South East. Clearly the availability of data will be important, but the monitoring system must be robust and capable of addressing adverse impacts of the strategy and changes in national policy. Monitoring information should be used both to determine whether the policies in this guidance are being implemented and whether they may need to be reviewed. It is, therefore, important that monitoring activity is consistent across local authority boundaries.

13.7   The Government has asked regions to prepare Sustainable Development Frameworks, which are high-level statements of regional vision for moving towards sustainable development and will include regional indicators and targets. Regional Chambers, Regional Development Agencies, local authorities, business networks, the voluntary sector, other public services and the Government Offices are involved in the preparation of these frameworks and the formulation of targets, for example with regard to renewable energy. These frameworks will inform subsequent reviews and sustainability appraisals of both RPG9 and the regional economic strategies and will help to inform the design and organisation of future regional monitoring systems.

13.8   This guidance identifies potential key targets and indicators as the basis for a future monitoring system. These include both contextual and output indicators. It will be the responsibility of SERPLAN and subsequently the future Regional Planning Bodies and Mayor of London to agree with the relevant Government Offices the design and organisation of the monitoring system and the frequency and form of reporting. The counties of Bedfordshire, Hertfordshire and Essex will, in future, be involved in the monitoring arrangements in the East of England. The regular monitoring of this guidance may suggest new indicators which should also be considered.

Policy MON1

Regular and effective monitoring of regional circumstances should be undertaken, involving the use of targets and indicators to measure the effectiveness of policies.

a   Regional Planning Bodies should consider and agree with the relevant Government Offices and other regional partners, the arrangements for monitoring, taking account of this guidance, targets and indicators identified in Sustainable Development Frameworks and other relevant targets.

b   the Mayor of London will be expected to produce an annual monitoring report taking into account guidance in Circular 1/2000 (*Strategic Planning in London*), RPG3, (prior to issue of Spatial Development Strategy) and PPG11 *(Regional Planning)*.

c   The following table can help to inform the design of future monitoring activity:

Chapter	Potential targets and aspects for which regional targets should be defined	Potential indicators and types of indicators
Quality of Life in Town and Country	At least 60% of all development to be on previously developed land and through conversion of existing buildings in ROSE.	% of development on previously developed land. Quantity on previously developed land suitable for development. Derelict land.
	Secure at least 30-50 dwellings per hectare net in ROSE.	Housing units per hectare.
	Make best use of existing properties.	Vacant properties. Unfit homes.
	Year on year reduction in rates of crime.	Selected crime rates.
	Improve the health of the population overall.	Expected years of healthy life.
	Year on year, improvement in provision of, or access to, key services in rural parishes.	% of rural parishes with access to key services.
Environmental Strategy and the Countryside	No net loss or damage to designated sites of international, national or strategic importance through developments.	Number and areas of designated sites affected.
	Year on year increase in each key habitat.	Area of each key habitat for which UK Biodiversity Action Plan (BAP) and local BAPs are prepared.
	Increase woodland area in ROSE from 11% to 15% by 2016.	Area of woodland.
	Increase public access and enjoyment of the countryside.	Access to the countryside.
	Year on year improvements in pollution levels.	Air and noise pollution levels.
The Regional Economy	Year on year reduction in disparities between economic performance of different parts of the Region.	GDP per capita.
	Maintain high and stable levels of employment.	Employment rates or % jobs in selected key sectors. Unemployment rates by district.
	Increase skills levels.	Qualification levels.
Housing	Sufficient housing.	Indicators to be developed e.g. • housing need (according to local authority waiting lists and registers of statutory homeless) • ratio of house prices to wage levels • mix of type and size of dwelling.

Chapter	Potential targets and aspects for which regional targets should be defined	Potential indicators and types of indicators
Housing (continued)	Sufficient affordable housing units.	Number of affordable homes completed each year compared with provisional regional indicator of 18,000-19,000 affordable units per annum in ROSE (to be updated on the basis of local need assessments).
	60% of all new housing to be on previously developed land and through conversions of existing buildings in ROSE by 2008.	% of housing on previously developed land.
Sustainable Transport	Reduce road congestion on the inter-urban network and in urban areas below current levels by 2010. Increase rail by 50% and bus use by 10% from 2000 levels by 2010. Reduce annual rate of increase in car traffic and, in urban areas, aim for absolute reductions in private motorised traffic. Achieve a one-third increase in the proportion of households in rural areas within about 10 minutes walk of an hourly or better bus service by 2010. Triple by 2010 the number of cycling trips compared with a 2000 base.	Ongoing work to develop appropriate indicators, e.g: • trip lengths by journey purpose; • modal splits by journey purpose; • public transport patronage.
	Reduce the number of people killed or seriously injured in road accidents by 40% by 2010 and the number of children by 50% compared with the average for 1994-98.	Casualties (by severity).
Development and the Supply of Infrastructure	Reduce the amount of municipal waste landfilled. Increase the proportion of household waste or sewage sludge recycled or composted.	Recycling and composting rates % of municipal waste diverted from landfill.
	Balance demand and supply of water.	As monitored by Environment Agency and Ofwat.
	Increase amount of electricity derived from renewable sources.	% of electricity derived from renewable sources.
Mineral Resource and Other Development	Year on year increase in use of recycled and secondary aggregates.	Sale of secondary and recycled aggregates and totals of these sold as a percentage of all aggregates sold. % of aggregates recycled. Number of aggregates recycling sites.

Updating and Reviewing Regional Planning

13.9 PPG11 *(Regional Planning)* advises that Regional Planning Guidance may be subject to selective or comprehensive review. Future reviews of RPG 9 will be carried out by the new Regional Planning Bodies for the South East and East of England regions and the Mayor of London on the basis of their boundaries which are the same as Government Office boundaries.

13.10 However, there will be a continuing need to co-ordinate planning across the broader South East area, to take account in particular of the relationship between London and the surrounding areas. In addition the Regional Planning Bodies and the Mayor will need to collaborate in monitoring the implementation of this RPG and in carrying out the further studies and additional work recommended. Pan regional co-ordination arrangements have been agreed between the Greater London Authority and the new Regional Planning Bodies for the South East and East of England regions.

13.11 The Secretary of State expects early reviews of this RPG particularly in respect of:

- transport, particularly the success of the parking strategy, the need to devise a more regionally specific ports policy and to update the Regional Transport Strategy following the completion of current transport studies;

- minerals, particularly in view of the proposed update of MPG6 *(Guidelines for Aggregates Provision in England)*;

- waste, in view of the advice in PPG10 *(Planning and Waste Management)* on the development of regional strategies for waste management and the need to set regional targets;

- tourism provision, including sport and recreation, in the light of regional tourism and cultural strategies;

- retail strategy in accordance with guidance in PPG11 *(Regional Planning)*;

- renewable energy, to deliver regional renewable energy targets once these have been defined;

- monitoring system, as result of the completion of the Sustainable Development Frameworks, relevant national advice and consideration of the operational arrangements.

13.12 Other aspects of the strategy may require review subject to the outcome of monitoring. It will be particularly important to monitor the adequacy of the housing provision set out in chapter 8 as part of the plan, monitor, manage approach. The Regional Planning Bodies and the Mayor of London should agree with the relevant Government Offices the appropriate indicators to be used for these purposes and should submit regular reports on the adequacy of housing provision. In parallel, local housing need assessments will be undertaken and studies of urban capacity and also studies of the potential growth areas. The Secretary of State expects advice at least every five years, sooner if necessary, to enable a review of the amount and distribution of housing provision in this guidance.

13.13 It will be important that further updates and reviews of this guidance involve participation by regional stakeholders. PPG11 *(Regional Planning)* provides further advice. For example, local health economies - Health Authorities, National Health Service (NHS) Trusts and Primary Care Groups and Trusts - as well as Regional Offices of the NHS Executive, are key stakeholders. In developing the guidance for the South East and East of England, the strategic links with local Health Improvement Programmes will need to be taken into account, as well as the support of Health Action Zone activity and the role of the NHS Executive Regional Offices in supporting health impact assessment work.

Maps

Map 1 - The South East Region in context

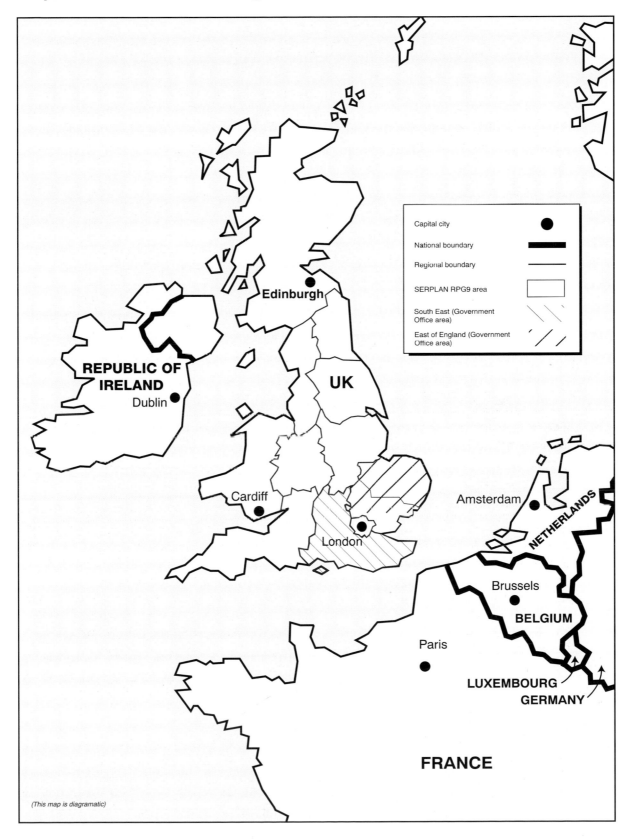

Capital city	●
National boundary	━━━
Regional boundary	───
SERPLAN RPG9 area	☐
South East (Government Office area)	
East of England (Government Office area)	

Edinburgh

REPUBLIC OF IRELAND

Dublin

UK

Cardiff

London

Amsterdam

NETHERLANDS

Brussels

BELGIUM

Paris

LUXEMBOURG

GERMANY

FRANCE

(This map is diagramatic)

Map 2 - Core Strategy

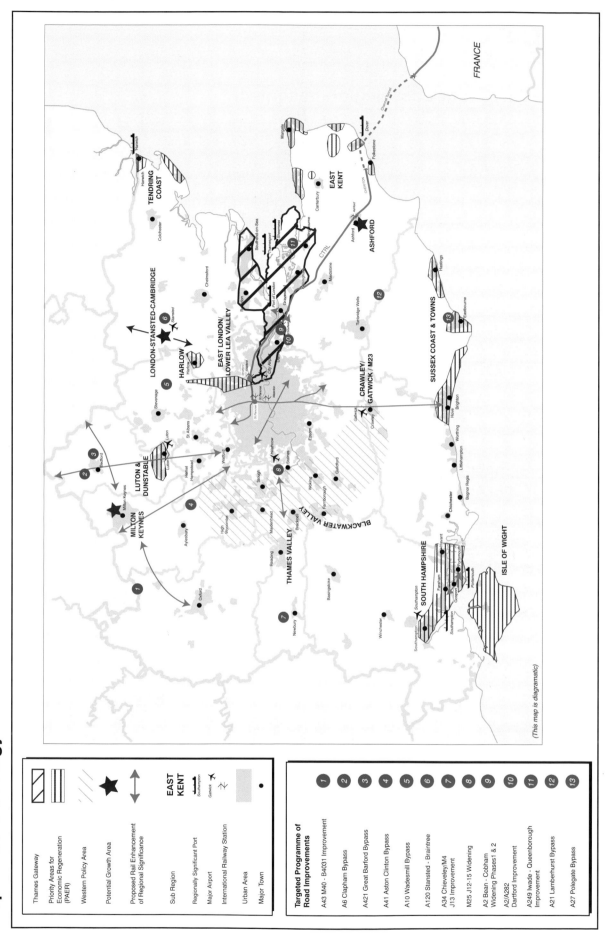

Legend:

Thames Gateway

Priority Areas for Economic Regeneration (PAER)

Western Policy Area

Potential Growth Area

Proposed Rail Enhancement of Regional Significance

Sub Region   EAST KENT

Regionally Significant Port   Southampton

Major Airport   Gatwick

International Railway Station

Urban Area

Major Town

Targeted Programme of Road Improvements

1. A43 M40 - B4031 Improvement
2. A6 Clapham Bypass
3. A421 Great Barford Bypass
4. A41 Aston Clinton Bypass
5. A10 Wadesmill Bypass
6. A120 Stansted - Braintree
7. A34 Chieveley/M4 J13 Improvement
8. M25 J12-15 Widening
9. A2 Bean - Cobham Widening Phases 1 & 2
10. A2/A282 Dartford Improvement
11. A249 Iwade - Queenborough Improvement
12. A21 Lamberhurst Bypass
13. A27 Polegate Bypass

(This map is diagramatic)

104

Map 3 - Communications (Studies)

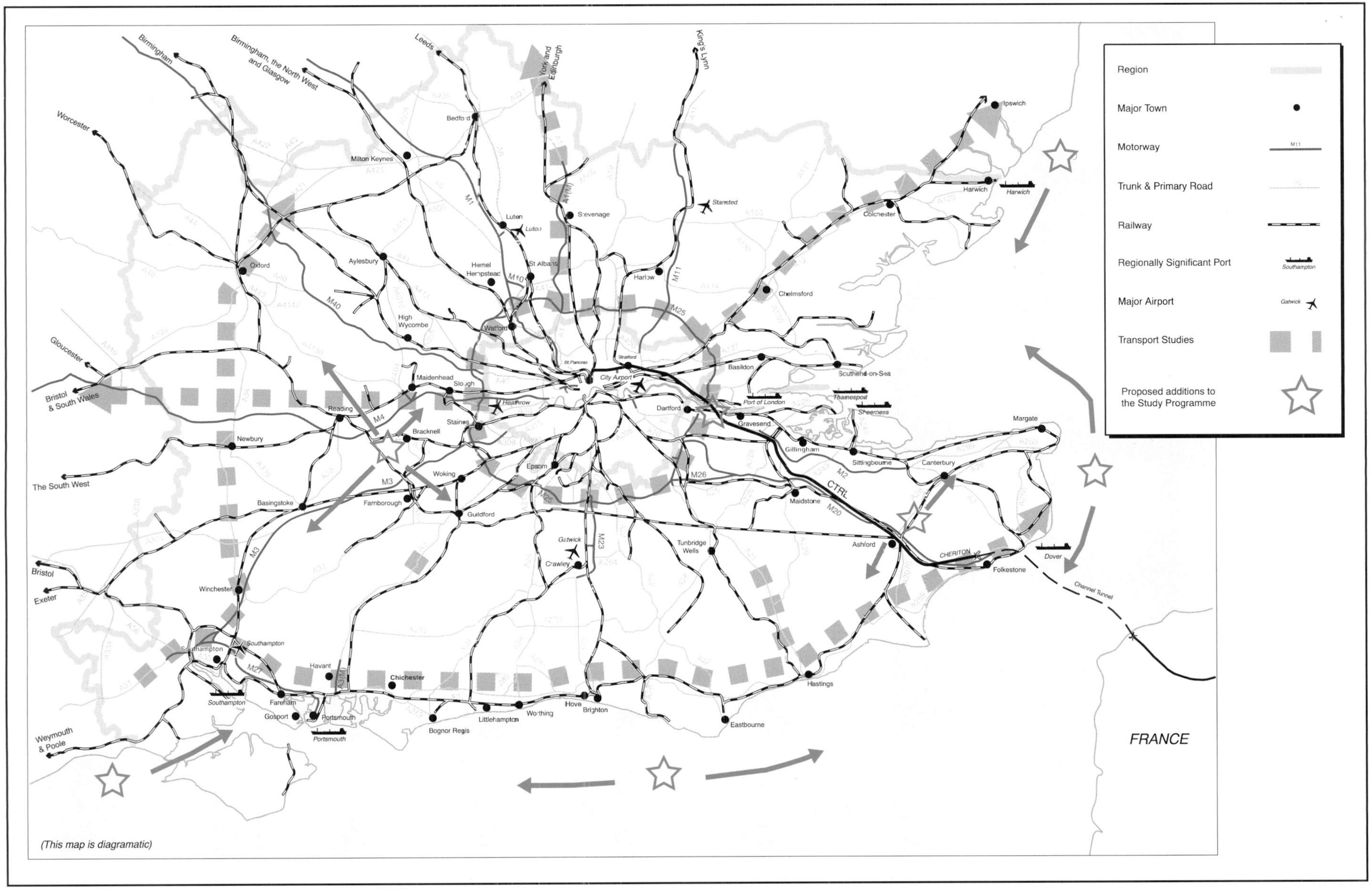

	Region
•	Major Town
M11	Motorway
	Trunk & Primary Road
	Railway
Southampton	Regionally Significant Port
✈ Gatwick	Major Airport
	Transport Studies
☆	Proposed additions to the Study Programme

(This map is diagramatic)

Map 4 - Environment

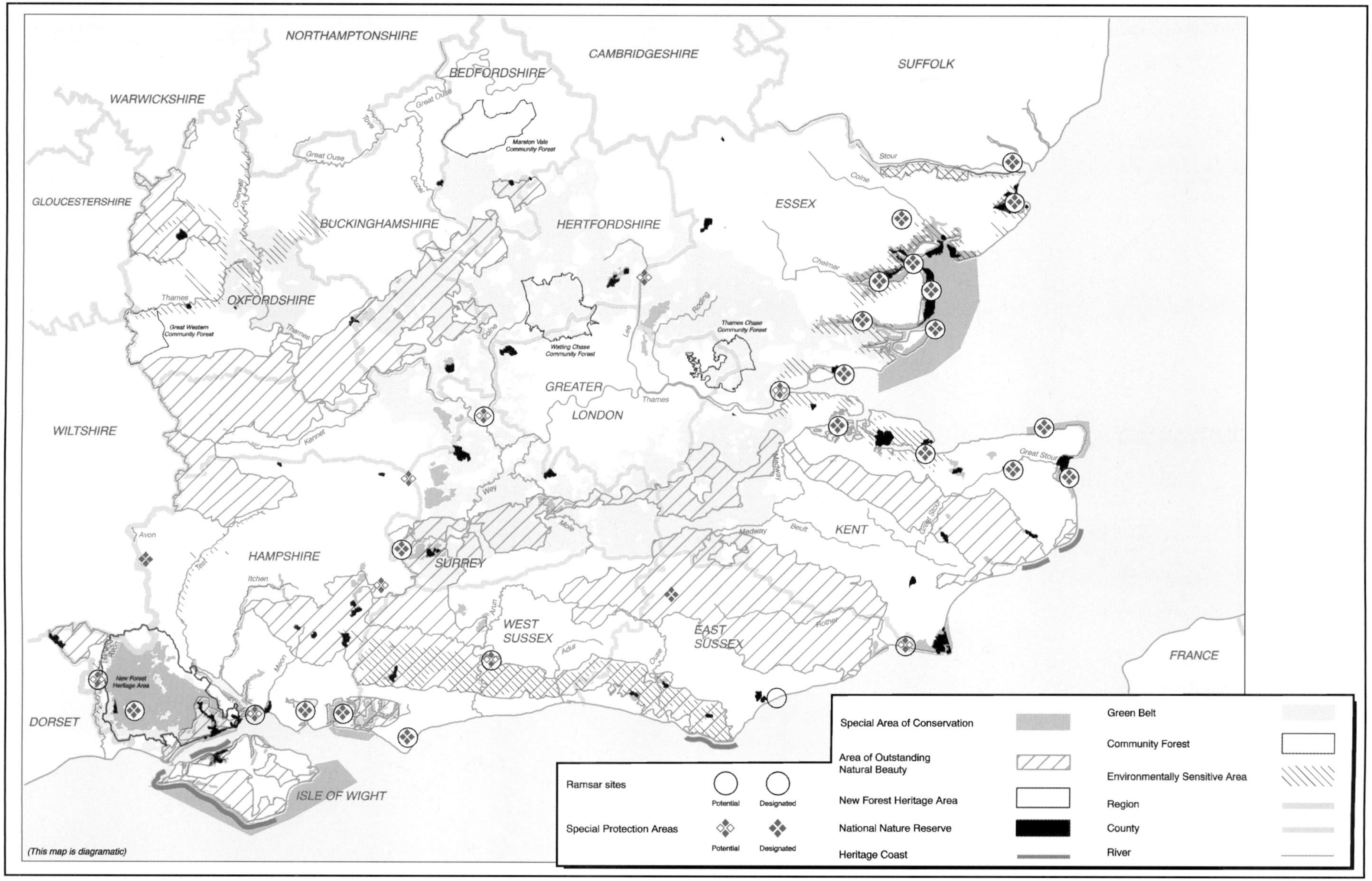

SUFFOLK

ESSEX

CAMBRIDGESHIRE

NORTHAMPTONSHIRE

BEDFORDSHIRE

HERTFORDSHIRE

GREATER LONDON

BUCKINGHAMSHIRE

OXFORDSHIRE

WARWICKSHIRE

GLOUCESTERSHIRE

WILTSHIRE

HAMPSHIRE

SURREY

WEST SUSSEX

EAST SUSSEX

KENT

DORSET

ISLE OF WIGHT

FRANCE

Stour

Colne

Chelmer

Thames

Lee

Great Ouse

Great Ouse

Ouzel

Tove

Cherwell

Thames

Thames

Kennet

Colne

Wey

Mole

Medway

Medway

Great Stour

River Stour

Beult

Rother

Ouse

Cuckmere

Arun

Adur

Avon

Itchen

Test

Avon

Itchen

Stour

Thames Chase Community Forest

Watling Chase Community Forest

Marston Vale Community Forest

Great Western Community Forest

New Forest Heritage Area

(This map is diagramatic)

Legend

Ramsar sites — Potential ○ / Designated ○

Special Protection Areas — Potential ◆ / Designated ◆

Special Area of Conservation

Area of Outstanding Natural Beauty

New Forest Heritage Area

National Nature Reserve

Heritage Coast

Green Belt

Community Forest

Environmentally Sensitive Area

Region

County

River

Map 5 - Economic Development

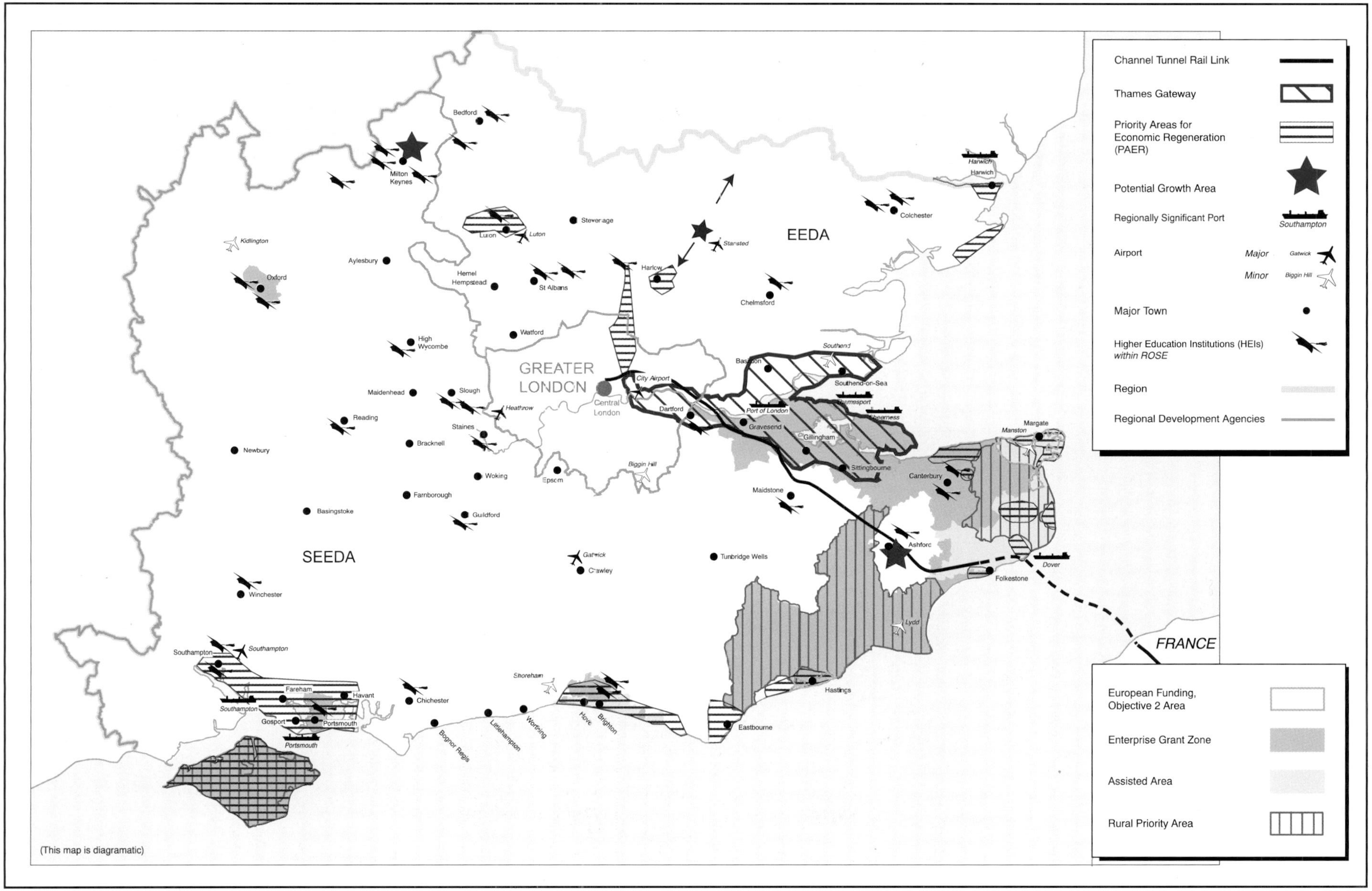

Legend:

- Channel Tunnel Rail Link
- Thames Gateway
- Priority Areas for Economic Regeneration (PAER)
- Potential Growth Area
- Regionally Significant Port *Southampton*
- Airport — *Gatwick* Major, *Biggin Hill* Minor
- Major Town
- Higher Education Institutions (HEIs) *within ROSE*
- Region
- Regional Development Agencies

- European Funding, Objective 2 Area
- Enterprise Grant Zone
- Assisted Area
- Rural Priority Area

FRANCE

EEDA

GREATER LONDON

SEEDA

Central London

Towns and places:
Harwich, Colchester, Chelmsford, Stansted, Harlow, Stevenage, Luton, St Albans, Watford, Hemel Hempstead, Bedford, Milton Keynes, Aylesbury, High Wycombe, Maidenhead, Reading, Basingstoke, Newbury, Oxford, Kidlington, Winchester, Southampton, Fareham, Havant, Gosport, Portsmouth, Chichester, Bognor Regis, Littlehampton, Worthing, Shoreham, Hove, Brighton, Crawley, Gatwick, Biggin Hill, Epsom, Heathrow, Slough, Staines, Bracknell, Farnborough, Woking, Guildford, City Airport, Dartford, Gravesend, Port of London, Basildon, Southend, Southend-on-Sea, Sheerness, Gillingham, Maidstone, Sittingbourne, Canterbury, Margate, Manston, Dover, Folkestone, Ashford, Lydd, Hastings, Eastbourne, Tunbridge Wells

(This map is diagramatic)

Map 6 - Administrative Areas

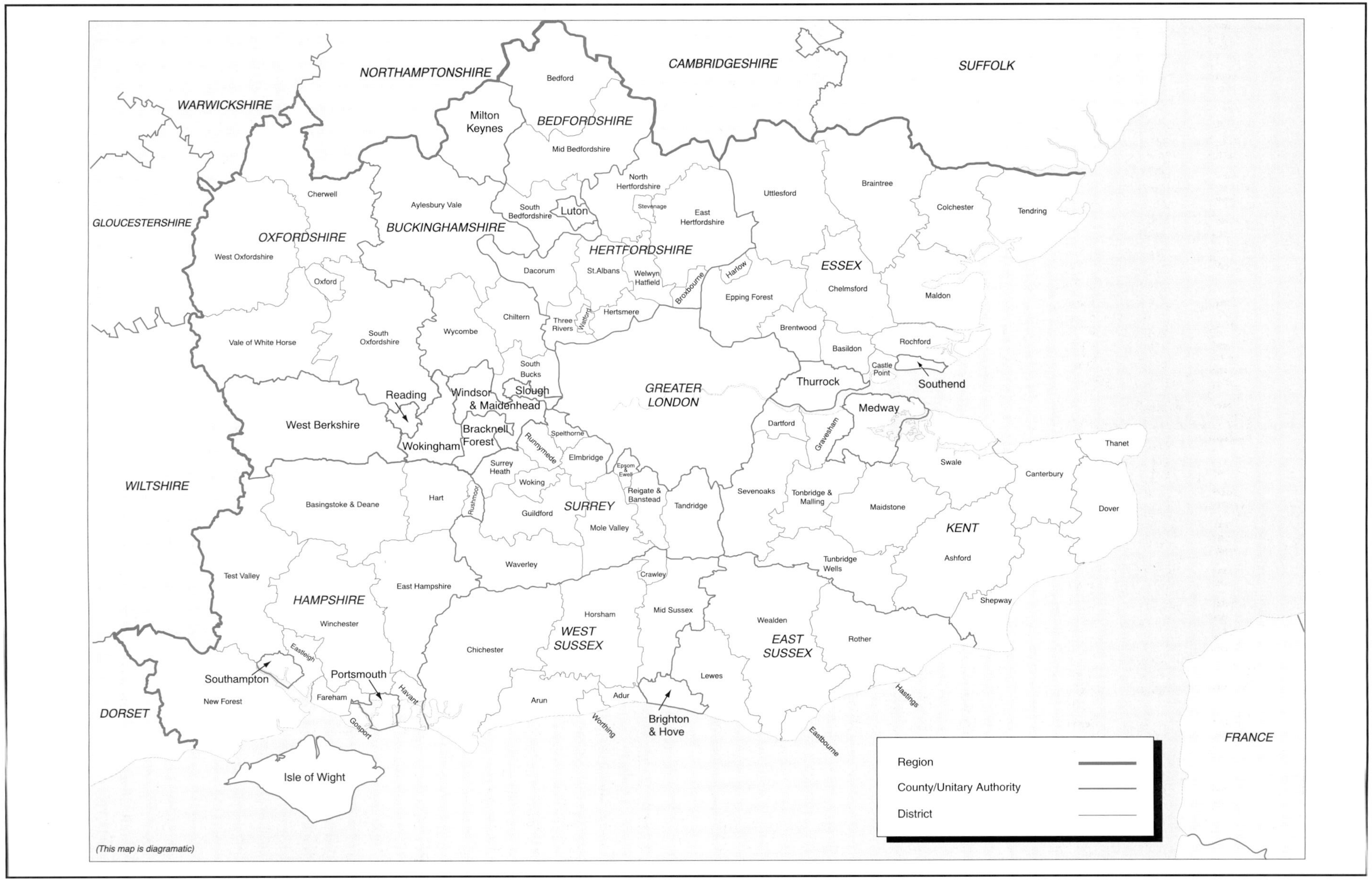

FRANCE

Legend:
Region
County/Unitary Authority
District

SUFFOLK

Thanet
Dover
Canterbury
Shepway
Ashford
KENT
Swale
Maidstone
Tonbridge & Malling
Tunbridge Wells
Rother
Sevenoaks
Hastings
EAST SUSSEX
Wealden
Eastbourne
Lewes
Tandridge
Mid Sussex
Brighton & Hove
Adur
Crawley
Worthing
Reigate & Banstead
Epsom & Ewell
Horsham
WEST SUSSEX
Mole Valley
SURREY
Arun
Guildford
Chichester
Waverley
Elmbridge
Woking
Spelthorne
Runnymede
Surrey Heath
Rushmoor
Hart
East Hampshire
Havant
Portsmouth
Gosport
Fareham
HAMPSHIRE
Winchester
Eastleigh
Isle of Wight
Southampton
New Forest
Test Valley
Basingstoke & Deane
DORSET
WILTSHIRE
West Berkshire
Reading
Wokingham
Bracknell Forest
Windsor & Maidenhead
Slough
South Bucks
Chiltern
Wycombe
South Oxfordshire
Vale of White Horse
Oxford
West Oxfordshire
Cherwell
OXFORDSHIRE
GLOUCESTERSHIRE
WARWICKSHIRE
NORTHAMPTONSHIRE
Milton Keynes
Aylesbury Vale
BUCKINGHAMSHIRE
Dacorum
Bedford
BEDFORDSHIRE
Mid Bedfordshire
South Bedfordshire
Luton
North Hertfordshire
Stevenage
St Albans
Three Rivers
Watford
Hertsmere
Welwyn Hatfield
East Hertfordshire
HERTFORDSHIRE
Broxbourne
Harlow
CAMBRIDGESHIRE
Epping Forest
Uttlesford
Braintree
Colchester
Maldon
Chelmsford
ESSEX
Brentwood
Basildon
Rochford
Southend
Castle Point
Thurrock
Dartford
Gravesham
Medway
Swale
GREATER LONDON

(This map is diagramatic)

Annex

List of Planning Policy Guidance Notes and Other Documents Referred to in the Text

PPG 1 .... General Policy and Principles (1997)

PPG 2 .... Green Belts (1995)

PPG 3 .... Housing (2000)

PPG 4 .... Industrial and Commercial Development and Small Firms (1992)

PPG 6 .... Town Centres and Retail Development (1996)

PPG 7 .... The Countryside - Environmental Quality and Economic and Social Development (1997)

PPG 8 .... Telecommunications (1992)

PPG 9 .... Nature Conservation (1994)

PPG 10 .... Planning and Waste Management (1999)

PPG 11 .... Regional Planning (2000)

PPG 12 .... Development Plans (2000)

PPG 13 .... Transport (Draft 1999)

PPG 14 .... Development on Unstable Land (1990)

PPG 14A .... Annex 1: Landslides and Planning (1996)

PPG 15 .... Planning and the Historic Environment (1994)

PPG 16 .... Archaeology and Planning (1990)

PPG 17 .... Sport and Recreation (1991)

PPG 18 .... Enforcing Planning Control (1991)

PPG 19 .... Outdoor Advertising Control (1992)

PPG 20 .... Coastal Planning (1992)

PPG 21 .... Tourism (1992)

PPG 22 .... Renewable Energy (1993)

PPG 23 .... Planning and Pollution Control (1994)

PPG 24 .... Planning and Noise (1994)

RPG 3 .... Strategic Guidance for London Planning Authorities (1996)

RPG3B/9B .... Strategic Planning Guidance for the River Thames (1997)

RPG 6 .... East Anglia - Draft Regional Planning Guidance - Proposed Changes (2000)

RPG 8 .... East Midlands

RPG 9A .... Thames Gateway Planning Framework (1995)

RPG 10 .... South West

RPG 11 .... West Midlands

MPG 1 .... General Considerations and the Development Plan System (1998)

MPG 6 .... Guidelines for the Aggregate Provision in England (1994)

MPG 7 .... The Reclamation of Mineral Workings

MPG 10 .... Provision of Raw Material for the Cement Industry (1991)

MPG 15 .... Silica Sand (1996)

Circular 1/97 ... Planning Obligations (1997)

Circular 6/98 ... Planning and Affordable housing (1998)

Government Office for London, Circular 1/2000 Strategic Planning in London

Department of Environment, Transport and the Regions, A Better Quality of Life: UK Sustainable Development Strategy (1999)

Department of Environment, Transport and the Regions, Towards an Urban Renaissance, Final Report of the Urban Task Force chaired by Lord Rogers of Riverside (1999)

Department of Environment, Transport and the Regions, Best Practice in Assessing Urban Housing Capacity (2000)

Department of Environment, Transport and the Regions, The National Cycling Strategy (1996)

Department of Environment, Transport and the Regions, A New Deal for Transport: Better for Everyone (1998)

Department of Environment, Transport and the Regions, A New Deal for Trunk Roads in England: Guidance on the New Approach to Appraisal (1998)

Department of Environment, Transport and the Regions, School Travel Strategies and Plans: A Best Practice Guide for Local Authorities (June 1999)

Department of Environment, Transport and the Regions, A Safer Journey to School (July 1999)

Department of Environment, Transport and the Regions, A Travel Plan Resource Pack for Employers (February 2000)

Department of Environment, Transport and the Regions, Guidance on Full Local Transport Plans (March 2000)

Department of Environment, Transport and the Regions, Transport 2010: The 10 Year Plan (October 2000)

Department of Environment, Transport and the Regions, Encouraging Walking: Advice to Local Authorities (March 2000)

Department of Environment, Transport and the Regions, The Air Quality Strategy for England, Scotland, Wales and Northern Ireland: Working Together for Clean Air (January 2000)

Department of Environment, Transport and the Regions, Building a Better Quality of Life: A Strategy for More Sustainable Construction (April 2000)

Department of Environment, Transport and the Regions, UK Biodiversity Action Plan (1999)

Department of Environment, Transport and the Regions, Waste Strategy 2000: England and Wales - Parts 1 & 2 (May 2000)

Department of Environment, Transport and the Regions, MPG 11 Controlling and Mitigating the Environmental Effects of Minerals Extraction in England (May 2000)

Department of Environment, Transport and the Regions, Controlling the Environmental Effects of Recycled and Secondary Aggregates Production: Good Practice Guidance (February 2000)

Department for Education and Employment, The Learning Age: A Renaissance for a New Britain (1998)

Department of Health, Saving Lives: Our Healthier Nation (1999)

Department of Transport, White Paper: Airports Policy (1985)

European Spatial Development Perspective (ESDP June 1998)

Forestry Commission, A New Focus for England's Woodlands: Strategic Priorities and Programmes - England Forestry Strategy

Government Office for the South East, Sustainable Residential Quality - New Approaches to Urban Living (Llewellyn Davies 1998)

Government Office for the South East, Sustainable Residential Quality in the South East (1998)

Government Office for the South East, Proposed Changes to Draft RPG9, and Reasons for the Proposed Changes (March 2000)

London Planning Advisory Committee, Sustainable Residential Quality - New Approaches to Urban Living (Llewellyn Davies 1998)

Ministry of Agriculture Fisheries and Food, England Rural Development Plan 2000 - 2006 (2000)

Ministry of Agriculture, Forestry and Fisheries, England Rural Development Plan (2000)

SERPLAN, Draft RPG9 - A Sustainable Development Strategy for the South East (1998)

Surrey County Council et al, Rising to the Challenge: Impacts of Climate Changes in the South East in the 21st Century (1999)

Sustainable Development, A Better Quality of Life: A Strategy for Sustainable Development in the UK (May 1999)